BREED

PUG

EDITED BY
NANCY TARBITT

ACKNOWLEDGEMENTS

The publishers would like to thank the following for help with photography: Daphne Crump (Pigalle); Elaine Passmore (Pelancy); Kay Cooper (?), Jason Hunt (Carpaccio); Jan Foster, Charlotte Patterson (Ivanwold), Carol Anne Giles (Coral Bay), Carolyn Koch (Chance Glory); Sabine Stuewer (www.stuewer-tierfoto.de); Hearing Dogs for Deaf People; Pets As Therapy.

Cover photo: © Tracy Morgan Animal Photography (www.animalphotographer.co.uk)

Dog fe_____ ___ J____ St_____ ___ _ by M__ G_ Garrard.

Pag__ ___ © www.comstock.com; Page 6 © Sabine Stuewer Tierfoto;
Page 13 © istoc_____ ___ j____ Hubert; Page 30 and 37 _____: Stuewer Tierfoto;
Page 50 © ist_____ kphoto.com_____ ____ _____ 12 istockphot___m/Carlsson Inc;
Page 5_ © ____ stock_photo.com/M___ ____ ___ ___ _____ ____ Tierfoto;
Page 60 © istoc__ photo.com/_____ ___ masti__ _____ ____/Anthony Gaudio;
Page 78 © Sabine Stuewer Tierfoto; Page 10_ © __gle_____ ____ ____athan Larsen;
Page 97 © istoc_____ hoto.com/Michael Mack___ Page 10_ ___ _____om/Mark Herreid;
Page 1_8 © www.comstock.com; Page 1__ © Sa____ _____ ___uewer Tierfoto.

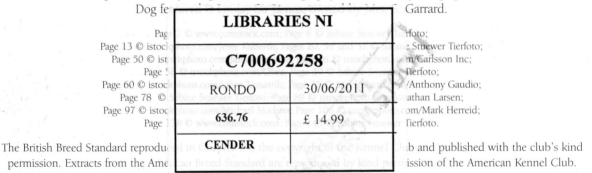

The British Breed Standard reprodu___ ___ ___ the copyright of the Kennel ___ub and published with the club's kind permission. Extracts from the Ame____an Breed Standard are r__p___ced by kind p___ission of the American Kennel Club.

THE QUESTION OF GENDER

The 'he' pronoun is used throughout this book instead of the rather impersonal 'it',
but no gender bias is intended.

First published in 2011 by The Pet Book Publishing Company Limited
PO Box 8, Lydney, Gloucestershire GL15 6YD

ISBN
978-1-906305-42-0
1-906305-42-0

Printed and bound in China by PWGS.

CONTENTS

GETTING TO KNOW THE PUG

Chapter 1

Getting to know your Pug will be an exciting time for dog and owners alike – and the experience will be enhanced by being aware of what you can expect from your new companion. The Pug is a small, smart dog, either black or fawn in colour, with a short, easy-to-care-for coat. He is both compact and sturdy, and his size and temperament will suit most homes. For centuries the Pug has lived as a beloved companion and all he asks for his affection and loyalty is to be loved in return and to play a big part in your life.

PHYSICAL CHARACTERISTICS

The Pug is classed as a Toy dog and although he is certainly small in size, he is by no means delicate. He is short and cobby in build, which means he should possess a well-balanced, nicely rounded body and have plenty of bone for his size. His construction should enable him to move soundly, with the typical Pug gait, which is often described as a Pug roll. He should have strong straight front legs, and a broad chest easing into a pleasing layback of shoulder, followed up with a level topline and firm, well-muscled hindquarters with a good bend of stifle, all topped up with his inimitable, well-curled tail held high on his back.

The Pug is known as one of the brachycephalic breeds. The word brachycephalic comes from the Greek roots: '**brachy**', meaning short, and '**cephalic**', meaning head. It is used to describe breeds with a short, broad muzzle; typically the breadth is at least 80 per cent of the length. As well as the Pug, there are a number of brachycephalic breeds, including the Boxer, the Bulldog, the Cavalier King Charles Spaniel, the Shih Tzu and the Pekingese. The construction of the head, with a shortened face and pushed-back nose, means these breeds are inefficient panters, and therefore susceptible to high temperatures. It is important to be fully aware of this when you are caring for your Pug.

The Pug's head should be on the large side and well wrinkled; the wrinkles should be well defined and, ideally, forming the desirable diamond shape on his forehead. His eyes should be big, dark and expressive, the expression ranging from dreamily thoughtful to full of fire, according to his mood at the time! Pugs can have either 'rose' ears or 'button' ears. A 'rose' ear is a small drop-ear that folds over and back. With a 'button' ear, the ear flap folds forward, and the tip lies close to the skull to cover the opening. In the show world,

BRAYCEPHALIC BREEDS

These breeds have short, broad muzzles and a wide head.

The Pug.

The Bulldog.

The Boxer.

The Cavalier King Charles Spaniel.

The Pekingese.

The Shih Tzu.

SNUFFLES AND SNORES

Another consequence of the 'pushed in' nose is that, inevitably, your Pug will snore a little. But to devoted Pug owners worldwide, who adore this soporific sound, this gentle but audible breathing is the signature of a normal, healthy Pug dog. It can be hard to keep awake if one has several Pugs ranged around one's feet, all happily snoozing away, piled in a heap together and snoring in different keys!

The Pug owner soon becomes familiar with the snuffles and snores of a sleeping Pug.

button ears are considered more desirable.

With proper care and the right feeding, the Pug puppy will grow into a compact little adult – very much *multum in parvo* – meaning he should be a 'lot in a little'. A mature adult, according to the Kennel Club guidelines, should finish at between 14 and 18 lbs, which is roughly between 6.5 and 8.5 kgs. Many a top-winning male in the show ring, however, will be above this weight, as good bone and well-developed muscle will make him weigh more than a bigger dog without these desirable attributes. The Pug should feel quite solid when picked up but must, above all, remain a quality little dog without the slightest hint of coarseness. His renowned curly tail is the first thing most people will notice – it should be set high on his back, carried proudly and nicely curled. A double twist is perfection!

COAT AND COLOUR

There are various shades of fawn, ranging from a creamy fawn to an apricot fawn; the significant contrast of jet-black pigmentation on his ears and muzzle is desirable along with shiny black toenails. A black Pug puppy should be as black as is possible, preferably displaying a close-fitting fine, single coat (this means that, unlike the fawn, he has no undercoat) and, most importantly, if you wish to show him, no white hairs.

TEMPERAMENT

The temperament of a typical little Pug is relaxed, self-confident and friendly. He is a little dog whose sole purpose in life is to please his owners. Should he appear to be uncooperative, it is more than likely that he has not come to grips with what is required of him. The Pug dog, being the great little character that he is, sometimes has a mind of his own and on occasion is smart enough to pretend not to realise what you want of him. For instance, if you call his name while he is intent on sniffing a particularly inviting smell, he may sometimes give the impression of being unable to hear you until ready to respond (in *his* time rather than yours…) when he will then bound towards you with a smile on his face saying:

"Sorry, I didn't hear you!"

Bred for generations to be a companion dog, the Pug's instinctive behaviour and, indeed, raison d'etre is to please. A mature Pug will sit alongside you, tune into your feelings and seem to listen to your worries. In short, they are totally happy just to be part of their owner's lives in the not-so-good times as well as the good, and they are the perfect breed for someone who requires companionship together with unquestionable loyalty.

The Pug's confident character can make him something of an attention-seeker; he is most content when basking in your attention and he will want to follow you around all day if at all possible. He is alert and will give warning if strangers approach his home, but is not a dog who barks

The Pug is a 'people dog" and thrives on spending time with his beloved family.

gratuitously, rather using his voice to communicate. He will always greet his family with rapture – even after the briefest absence – but may, initially, be a little wary with people he does not know well. This will take the form of waiting to see how things go before rushing in. He likes to assess the situation, which shows a degree of caution that has nothing to do with aggression.

Leaving a Pug on his own all day and every day is never to be recommended. This is a breed who, more than most dogs, absolutely thrives on human company, and while he may appear to prosper if left on his own, he will not thrive. He will never develop his true character and you will miss out on the unique bond that comes if you love him and spend lots of time in his company.

THE ADAPTABLE PUG

Pugs are extremely adaptable. They can be equally fulfilled by living with either a single person or several people, and quickly become valued family members. A Pug will fit in with a family or as the devoted companion of older people, content always to be there and willing to be quietly comforting if needed. He loves to be stroked and cuddled, and if his owner is stressed, this can be used as a great calming technique. The Pug is capable of leading an active life well into old age and has both the commitment and desire to join in with all but the most energetic of pursuits.

A SUITABLE HOME

As far as a Pug is concerned, the ideal home is one with a comfortable bed, where food is served at regular times in a warm, clean and, above all, loving environment where he is able to spend most of his time alongside the person he loves best and to give his whole being to that person. Rich or poor, town or country – it is all the same to him, providing he is with his loved ones and receives the necessary basic care and attention, plus enough exercise to keep him fit in both mind and body.

Access to a garden will make life easier and more enjoyable for both Pug and owner. If, for some reason, on the odd occasion a walk is not possible, he will be perfectly happy to amuse himself, playing in the garden for a short time, particularly so if he has a companion Pug or a child to be with. The majority of Pug owners may well consider a garden an essential requirement for dog

The adaptable Pug takes life in his stride and will be ready to fit in with his owner's lifestyle.

ownership, but I have seen Pugs living active, happy and healthy lives in a flat in the centre of London. In this situation, the need is for the Pug to have regular access to outdoor space several times a day and, preferably, somewhere where he can be off the lead safely for a short time without being vulnerable to traffic or to other dogs, who, in a communal space, may not be well disposed to him. It is comparatively easy, even in a city, to find a quiet corner of a park or some such place where he can happily snuffle around unrestricted, but safely under the watchful eye of his owner.

A SPECIAL RELATIONSHIP

These admirable little dogs are simply wonderful with children. At times I sometimes feel they can be a little too wonderful, as they will suffer being pulled around without complaint by an over-enthusiastic child who probably knows no better. Most Pugs seem to adore children and actively seek out contact with them, even including very young babies. This is particularly unusual, as many breeds of dog can be instinctively afraid of babies – maybe because of the odd noises they can make! The average Pug dog does not appear to be concerned by this, but is rather curious and positively relishes close proximity to his human family's toddlers. He appears to adjust his responses according to the age and capability of the child.

The Pug will actively seek out contact with children.

THE SOCIABLE PUG

Pugs have a special affinity with their own kind.

Children who have not been brought up with dogs can often be unaware that they are being over-exuberant, so you must always be ready to intervene if the game little Pug is being exhausted or run off his feet, as he will rarely complain.

When young, he is a playful, little dog who loves to interact with his owners. Most Pugs absolutely adore toys – mine have a huge basket of assorted playthings and, amazingly, will walk to it and spend a considerable time hunting for, and finally selecting, the toy they want and *know* is there, even if it takes ages to find it at the bottom of the basket.

Mutual respect of both dog and owner should be established when the Pug is young, with the puppy being made aware by your response that certain behaviour is not acceptable. This is easily and painlessly conveyed if you withdraw your attention for a very short period. I usually find that deliberately, and rather ostentatiously, turning my back and completely ignoring him for merely a few seconds is enough. Be quick to praise him over-lavishly for good behaviour, and very soon the little dog will acquire a standard of behaviour acceptable to you both, which will make life easier and more pleasant for all. The reverse side of the coin is that you must

Small breeds tend to be very collectable.

Mixing little and large can work well.

also be aware and respect *his* needs, too.

LIVING WITH OTHER DOGS

Pugs are extremely gregarious. They absolutely adore to be with their own kind and seem to recognise their own breed immediately when meeting in the park or out walking. To see several Pugs settling down in a heap together, or all snuffling happily round a garden *en masse* is a sight that can be unknown

in some other breeds. Put down several beds for eight or so Pugs and they will be found cramming themselves into one, leaving all the rest unoccupied.

The Pug will also live happily and without aggression with other compatible breeds, although you should always exercise care with larger or more challenging dogs until you can be absolutely sure of the Pug's safety. The Pug, by the very nature of his size and trusting

nature, can be very vulnerable to aggression by other dogs and animals, and should never be exposed to a situation where this is possible. However, I know of several households where a Pug lives contentedly alongside a dog who is considerably larger than him in size. Indeed, the Pug is more than capable of quietly taking over as the boss dog; he does not make a song and dance about it, but he is the one who ends up in control!

LIVING WITH SMALL ANIMALS

Being extremely tolerant in character, the Pug will quickly adjust to living alongside cats and other household pets with few problems encountered.

Obviously, precautions should be taken initially until both animals are accustomed to each other – particularly with a cat, as the Pug's largish eyes can make him susceptible to claw damage. Pugs and cats can and do become great friends, given time to adjust – in fact, I feel that there is something rather cat-like about the Pug. Whatever the reason, they can live contentedly alongside each other.

During my many years of living with Pugs, I was called upon at one time to hand-rear a baby squirrel. When tiring, this bushy-tailed little guy would boldly seek the company of a pile of sleeping Pugs, and actually snuggle in with them and be accepted without any of the Pugs turning a hair. I have noticed, when walking my dogs, that wild birds and other small creatures seem aware that the Pugs are no threat and show no fear of them.

CARE REGIME

A huge plus in the Pug's favour for most owners is his 'wash and go' coat texture, which makes him such an easy dog to care for and, thus, attractive to people of all ages. All that is required is an aware and alert owner, who is prepared to give him a few minutes of attention each day, checking over his nose wrinkles and ears, plus a quick brush and an occasional bath. This is all a Pug needs. Most Pugs actually enjoy bathtime; I bathe my dogs using the shower spray in an empty bath and a suitable mild shampoo, rinsing them off with plenty of warm water and wrapping them in a warm towel to dry them. I use the baby towels, with hoods, which keep the towel in place while the worst of the dampness is absorbed. My Pugs also enjoy drying themselves by running around the garden, shaking themselves in the sunshine, if the weather is kind.

EXERCISE

The Pug's exercise requirements are simple – several short walks per day being the ideal. A Pug can and will accompany his owner on longer walks, but too much should never be asked of him, as he remains a small dog who will often give more than he should for his own wellbeing in his desire to please. Be vigilant to when your Pug is tiring.

A puppy under six months of age should only ever be given gentle exercise – free play in the garden and very short walks under control on his lead will meet all his needs. Never, ever, walk your Pug in the heat of the day in warm weather. I cannot stress this too strongly. The short face that is typical of the breed makes it difficult for him to cope with high temperatures. Therefore, if the weather is at all warm or close, he should only be exercised in the cool of the early morning and again in the evening when the sun has lost most of its strength.

Leaving the Pug in a warm

A fit Pug will enjoy his exercise, particularly if he has the added stimulation of going to new places.

Do not under-estimate the intelligence of a Pug. He can be trained to a high standard.

The Pug may not get top marks in obedience – but there is no doubting he is smart.

place in the sun, particularly in a closed car, can be disastrous and will often result in fatality. A car soon heats up and the temperature becomes unbearable; death can occur in an amazingly short time – often in only a few minutes.

TRAINABILITY

The Pug is an easy little dog to train, although most owners are content with basic training, i.e. house training, walking on the lead without pulling, to sit on command, and a few other simple things that may go to make day-to-day living easier for both of you.

The Pug is an instinctively clean little dog, so puppies are usually very easy to house train. By the time they are ready to leave their birth home, they are usually accustomed to the use of either a puppy pad (which can be bought quite cheaply in packs and are much more hygienic) or newspaper placed in a strategic spot. Once in their new home it is then a simple task to move the pad a little nearer the door each day until the puppy gradually becomes accustomed to using the garden. House training should be well on the way by the time a puppy is four months of age, at which time he begins to acquire the ability and awareness to wait a short time until convenient for him to go outside. Teething may well interfere with house training for a time, but usually only for a short period until the offending

tooth has come through.

Introduce the collar indoors at first and only ever under supervision. A puppy should never be left alone while wearing his collar and, indeed, I am never happy to leave a collar on an unsupervised Pug of any age. The puppy will, undoubtedly, at first attempt to chew it and pull it off, and a typical reaction is for him to sit down initially and refuse to move. This stage will soon pass and as soon as the baby is accustomed to wearing his collar for short periods and the novelty of it has worn off, then is the time to introduce the lead.

Clip the lead on to his collar, while distracting him by telling him what a good, clever boy he is, and view his reaction. Any initial pulling or sitting down that takes place can be countered by allowing him to drag his lead around for a minute or two (still fastened to his collar and under supervision), until he becomes accustomed to the feeling. Once he is content to wear the collar and move with you holding the lead, then is the time to venture out of doors, in a quiet place at first, and only venturing together into public places when he becomes more skilled and assured.

The Pug, by nature of his build and temperament, is not a natural when it comes to competing in canine sports.

However, I well recollect seeing photographs of a little black Pug merrily leaping over small hurdles when taking part in agility. This is something that some Pugs may do, but I suggest it may well be the exception rather than the rule. Most Pugs, especially males, are willing enough to try anything within their capabilities, and if you aspire to competing with your Pug then there is certainly no harm in seeing if this is something you and your little dog would enjoy doing together.

For more information, see Chapter Six: Training and Socialisation.

ASSISTANCE DOGS

Maybe the Pug would not be the first breed to come to mind when thinking of dogs that help their owners in this way, but I am sure there are many Pugs who fulfil the function of assistance dogs without any formal training. Their owners may be completely unaware of the fact that the Pug is actually functioning as such, and is doing so as an extension of his loving and inborn desire to please.

HEARING DOGS

The Pug is an alert, little dog, which makes him ideal to work as a hearing dog, assisting

LIFE EXPECTANCY

Like many of the Toy dogs, the Pug is a long-lived breed – but it is difficult to be accurate about their longevity as so much depends on lifestyle. I have owned Pugs for well over 40 years now, and I think it would be correct to say that, while 11 years of age is the average length of life for a Pug, it is not at all uncommon for a well-cared-for Pug to live well beyond this.

My own longest-lived Pug was just over 15 years old when she died. She had been born with a cleft palate and was given to me at three days old in the hope I could hand-rear her. I did, against all the odds, and she became the love of my life – a feisty, adorable little Pug who had considerable attitude. Although she never weighed much over 4 kgs, she would eat for England, given the chance, and lived her life to the full.

I personally know of quite a few Pugs who have lived to be 17 years, and I have heard of one living to be almost 20 – but I would say these are the exceptions rather than the rule.

THERAPY DOGS

With their affectionate temperaments and great love of attention, Pugs positively thrive on being stroked and petted, and are, thus, tailormade to be successful therapy dogs. Dogs of all breeds are used worldwide to visit hospitals and residential care homes to bring comfort to those who are deprived of the companionship of animals. In many cases, a patient or elderly resident may have had to part with a pet they could no longer care for, so they greatly appreciate the chance to interact with a well-trained therapy dog.

In the UK, the organisation for therapy dogs is known as PAT (Pets as Therapy) dogs, and it recruits volunteers nationwide who have dogs that are suitable for this type of work. Before starting visits, every dog is given an assessment to check that he is well behaved, bombproof in all situations, and is ready to accept the attention of strangers. Visits are also organised to schools, and therapy dogs do valuable work helping children to learn how to interact with them, as well as providing a huge talking point, which is especially important for children with learning disabilities.

The Pug has so much to offer in this field: he is so full of character, so affectionate, and although he is small, he is sturdy enough to accept a lot of handling from different people.

An affectionate nature makes the Pug an ideal candidate for Therapy work.

those with hearing disabilities. Hearing dogs are trained to listen out for specific household sounds, such as the telephone, the doorbell, an alarm clock, an oven timer, and a smoke alarm, and then alert their owner. The dog will do this by physical contact, such as reaching up with a paw, and will then lead the owner to the sound. This makes daily life so much easier for a person with hearing disabilities, and on more than one occasion, a dog has saved his owner's life by alerting them to danger.

SUMMING UP
The Pug is a very special breed the following lines sum him up:

Pugs are perfect companion dogs

Uniquely beautiful to those who love them

Gregarious in a way few other breeds are – and thoroughly

Special – love a Pug and you have a friend for life!

THE FIRST PUGS

Chapter 2

Factual information on the origins of the Pug does not really exist, so we have to accept what anecdotal information is available and the weight of expert opinion, which favours China.

CHINESE ROOTS

The Chinese were regarded as a civilised society long before Europeans, and were breeding dogs on a state-organised basis as early as the 12th century BC. The imperial palaces were heavily involved with these activities right up to the 20th century. In the period 700 to 600BC, there were reports of short-faced, sporting dogs, so it is not impossible that the ancestor of the Pug dog was from among these breeds, but it was not until about AD100 that types of dogs were given names.

The field now narrows to the Szuchuan province of China where the breeding of the smaller and short-faced breeds was refined. There were four breeds that are of interest to us. Two were fawns with black marks; the larger being the Chinese Mastiff and the smaller being the Lo-tze (Chinese Pug). Both were regarded as old breeds with, perhaps, the Lo-tze being the older. Other than size, their similarities suggested they may even have had a common ancestor. The other two breeds were the Pekingese and Japanese Spaniel, which came in mixed colours and were thought to have started as long-nosed breeds whose faces were shortened over a long period with selective breeding. The first two breeds pre-dated the latter.

It was at this time that the first overland trade route was established westward and, no doubt, as well as expensive silks, some equally valuable Lo-tzes made the perilous journey. It was not until AD732 that the first Szuchuan Pai Dog (or Lo-tze) was officially recorded as being sent from Korea to the Japanese Emperor. In the period AD970-1150, Lo-tzes of varying colours were being reported and we might well be tempted to speculate that the Black Pug dates from this time. The painting in the *Imperial Dog Book* gives us both the appearance of the Lo-tze (Chinese Pug) and the colour black.

With the Chinese entering into a period of isolation, there is little or no news until sea trade was established between Canton and Portugal in 1516, together with their close allies, Spain. It comes as a little surprise to learn that Lo-tzes (or Chinese Pugs) became favourites with noble Spanish ladies. They were referred to in court circles as 'Isabellean' a name used to describe their fawn coat.

EARLY ORIGINS

The Lo-tze (Chinese Pug) from *The Imperial Dog Book*.

A 17th century illustration shows the breed taking on a Mastiff shape.

Mops and Nell: The foundation stock of the Willoughby Pugs.

THE DUTCH CONNECTION

In the 16th century, the Netherlands were ruled by Spain and were busily engaged in their struggle for independence. In 1572, William the Silent, more formally known as William I, Prince of Orange, was in possession of a Pug dog named Pompey, possibly obtained from the Spanish court.

The story goes that a party of Spanish assassins were approaching his tent at the dead of night when he was awoken by Pompey's barking and escaped to safety. We will never know how much truth there is in this story, but it seems to have been a pivotal point in the history of the Pug, for it had now become established in the House of Orange and has since remained the darling of both royalty and nobility.

When the Dutch gained their independence, they established their own trading with China in 1602, which became known as the Dutch East India Company. No doubt this meant that more Pugs were imported from China from time to time, for they were still court favourites when William and Mary came to the British throne in 1688, bringing their Pugs with them.

By this time, Pugs had evolved into a European equivalent of the Chinese Pug, and were originally known as Dutch Mastiffs. Looking at the illustration of a Pug around the seventeenth century, it is easy to see why the word 'Mastiff' appeared in its name.

There are reports of the Pug being very popular in Spain and Italy, as well as fawns and blacks being freely available in eighteenth century Russian markets, but we hear little of its progress in Britain apart from its appearance in paintings or other work of art. However, the Pug was to find royal favour first with George II and Queen Caroline, then with George III (and Queen Charlotte, who became an ardent breeder and admirer of Pugs. Both Georges have featured in paintings with their Pugs. After a brief interlude, covering the reigns of George IV and William IV, they emerged again as favourites in Queen Victoria's Windsor kennels, which helped them to become the most popular Toy dogs of the Victorian era. In more recent times, they were the darlings of the Duke and Duchess of Windsor.

DARK DAYS

The first half of the nineteenth century was the darkest of times for our Pugs. They were cruelly used with the bull breeds in an effort to reduce size and shorten faces in those breeds. The breeders' efforts were never very successful, but there were many awful mongrel Pugs left over to tell the tale. To add insult to injury, ear cropping was widely used by Pug owners to enhance the dogs' appearance. It is very difficult for us now to consider those early Pugs as beautiful – even if it was not illegal. None of us would consider subjecting our dogs to such pain and discomfort.

BREED PIONEERS

No doubt, the breed would have slowly evolved in the hands of the small, dedicated breeder, but suddenly two influential breeders arrived from completely different backgrounds.

In 1850, Lord Willoughby d'Eresby arrived on the scene with his parent stock, Mops and Nell. It is said that he imported Pugs from the continent, but it is from this named pair onwards that we can trace bloodlines with any certainty. The overall appearance seems to have changed little from the seventeenth-century specimens, except that these have cropped ears. We are most fortunate that so much Pug and family history is available to us in the collection at Grimsthorpe Castle, Lincolnshire.

Again, around 1850, Chas Morrison appeared with his pair of Pugs, named Punch and Tetty. Detailed information about Morrison remains elusive; we know only that he was proprietor of an inn at Walham Green, Fulham. He is said to have obtained his stock by 'backstairs' methods from royalty.

From the illustration of his parent stock, Punch and Tetty, there seems little physical difference from Mops and Nell.

WHAT'S IN A NAME?

From the fifteenth century, the name Pug or Pugge was used to describe monkeys, which were kept as pets. In the seventeenth century the term began to be used for a monkey or a dog, and later was used for the Pug dog only.

An alternative derivation was suggested by the Victorian author Idstone (the Reverend Pearce). He believed that it was derived from the Greek from whence came the Latin 'Pugnus' because the shadow of a clenched fist was considered to resemble the dog's profile. Perhaps both are true!

The essential difference was in the colour. The Willoughby strain had 'salt and pepper' colouring with some dark patches, whereas Morrison's strain was golden fawn. Eventually cross-breeding took place and subsequent stock began to enjoy the attributes of both sets of parents.

It is difficult to proceed further without a look at the show scene of the nineteenth century. Initially roadhouses (inns) were heavily involved with dog fighting and many other dubious activities. However, times were changing and the men who bred dogs for fighting started to look for other ways to prove their quality. Slowly, the small shows staged at the roadhouses developed into large, organised dog shows that were held annually. Birmingham was one of these early shows, and in 1860 they included a special

class for Pugs. Alas, there were no entries but soon the idea caught on and there were Pug entries, such as Blondin, appearing among the winners. It could well be that the attempts to breed dogs that could win at such shows accelerated the development of the modern Pug.

In the middle to late 1860s, with increasingly respectable and well-run shows becoming the

Wood carving of Punch and Tetty, owned by Chas Morrison.

23

BREED PIONEERS

Mrs M.A. Foster, the first great breeder and exhibitor of Pugs.

Mrs James Lindsay with Ch. Tum Tum.

norm, ladies started to get involved in breeding and exhibiting. The first great Pug breeder and exhibitor was Mrs M. A. Foster of Bradford, who won more than 10,000 prizes during her active participation. She bred and campaigned homebred Champions Jenny, Lovat, Luna, Diamond and Bradford Ruby.

At this time, we also had the appearance of Mrs Laura Mayhew of Twickenham. She introduced Chinese blood directly into her stock by mating Lamb with Moss (both Chinese imports). Click by Lamb out of Moss must be the most widely known mating ever in our breed.

BIRTH OF THE KENNEL CLUB

In 1871 legislation in favour of the dog was first introduced, and this was closely followed by the formation of the Kennel Club in April 1873. Many of the regulations introduced by the club were not popular but were accepted for the general good. The most significant changes to the show scene were the introduction of registrations and meaningful pedigrees, all recorded in their stud book which was published annually. Identification was further aided by the introduction of the breeder's affix.

In addition, the Kennel Club published a list of shows annually, which were held under their rules, and those that counted towards a "two-tier Champion" qualification. The number and standard of wins to become a Kennel Club Champion was also laid down.

The Kennel Club published a list of approved shows annually. Up until 1896 these classes counted towards Championship qualification. A candidate would first need to complete four class wins, then three Champion class wins, one of which had to be held at either the Birmingham or Kennel Club shows. In 1896 Challenge Certificates were introduce at these shows. The early results are not all available, but later they are complete and easy to follow.

THE FIRST CHAMPIONS
It took an exhibit some time to amass enough wins to gain a title. The first such Champion was a Pug made up in 1881. Comedy was a fawn dog owned, exhibited and bred by H. Maule of Leeds. He was sired by Tragedy out of Cloudy, who was the daughter of Click. The second relevant Champion, two years later, was Tum Tum II, who could similarly be traced back to Click. Again, in 1888, the outstanding Champion Loris could be traced back to Click. There are many more

Ch. Loris, made up in 1888.

examples traceable in this manner and, significantly, all tended to have shorter noses than previously. The result of introducing Chinese blood was there to be seen and, furthermore, the value of reliable pedigrees was increasingly evident. A head-study of Click is all we have available and, sadly, that is rather indistinct, but it gives some idea of what this highly influential Pug looked like.

The weight of exhibits was very important; classes had weight restrictions with judge's scales to enforce them. The early Champions tended to weigh from 13 to 15lbs (5.8-6.7 kgs). The two Champions, Tum Tum and Loris, certainly fell into this category. A top weight of 20 lbs (9 kgs) was the maximum allowed at the shows and any exhibit outside the weight limits

was automatically disqualified. Weight categories continued in our club shows until 1905 but no details are available on shows in general.

BLACK IS BEAUTIFUL
Lady Brassey, a noted breeder and exhibitor of the Victorian era, was a lady of immense talent and vigour. She had fawn Pugs and one fawn Champion, named Challenger, but her great passion was for black Pugs. This was unusual at that time, as black dogs were regarded by most breeders as rubbish and only fit to be consigned to the bucket. Lady Brassey amassed a number of good-quality blacks, some of which she brought back from China on her South Seas trip on the family yacht, *Sunbeam*. They were not the first or only blacks in Britain, but the significance

All black Pugs today are descended from Brassey stock.

FORMATION OF BREED CLUBS

The formation of the Kennel Club triggered a reaction in the breed enthusiasts and breed-specific clubs started to develop. The first was the Bulldog Club in 1875, and the ninth to be formed was the Pug Dog Club in 1883. One of the founder members was, of course, Mrs Mayhew, by now one of the influential Pug establishment. A set of rules was drawn up and an annual membership fee of one guinea set. More importantly, a list of breed points was established in an endeavour to maintain and hopefully improve standards.

The first Breed Standard was for fawns only. Nevertheless the quest for the Holy Grail was on – namely, the close-coupled Pug with a flat, wrinkled face, black mask, black velvety ears and a tightly curled tail.

Two years later, a show secretary was appointed and the first breed show was held at the Royal Aquarium, Westminster, in June 1885. Early dog shows were run on the same lines as horticultural shows and generally lasted three days. The first day was for collection and benching, the second for judging and the presentation of awards, and third day was open to the public. Exhibitors did not need to attend in person, as there was an excellent collection and delivery service run by the railways. The exhibiter delivered the exhibits to the local station in a suitable travelling cage. The show stewards

was that she had both the persistence and influence to persuade the establishment to introduce the first class specifically for black Pugs at the Maidstone show in 1886. All of the entries belonged to Lady Brassey.

Sadly, she died and was buried at sea the following year, but the scene was now set and although the first classes for blacks did not take place at breed club shows until 1890, black Pugs went from strength to strength. It is important to note that all of the great blacks that followed were descended from Brassey stock.

MAKING PROGRESS

The latter part of the 19th century was an extremely eventful period in the progress of the breed, as well as in the competitive arena of showing. In 1896 two dramatic changes occurred. Firstly, a petition submitted to the Kennel Club on behalf of owners and breeders of black Pugs by the redoubtable Mrs Stennard Robinson was successful, meaning blacks could now be registered in a separate category to fawns.

This had a very immediate impact as, in the same year, the system of qualification for the title Champion (now officially abbreviated to Ch.) would be governed by the award of Challenge Certificates (CCs), which were made available by the Kennel Club at General Championship Shows and approved breed club shows. This system is still in place today. Three CCs were required for a dog to become a Champion, each CC had to be awarded from a different judge.

The effect on the Pug-showing world was that there were now to be two sets of CCs available: one set for a fawn dog and a fawn bitch, and an additional set for a

would collect them, take them to the show, bench them, feed and water them for the duration of their stay, show them, and then deliver them back to the railway station. The owner would then collect them back from the local station. However, most serious exhibitors preferred to attend in person.

In 1887 Charles Cruft was appointed to the post of secretary in the first show where the Challenge Cup (known as the 20 Guinea Challenge Cup) was on offer. The first name ever to be engraved on a Pug trophy is Little Count. The cup is still on active service and can be seen to this day.

In 1888 Charles Cruft became honorary and show secretary of the club and remained so until he resigned to prepare and hold his own show at the Agricultural Hall, Islington, in 1891. We all know, of course, what a successful outcome that had.

Life is never straightforward and, due to geographical difficulties, a second club was formed in 1894. This was the Universal Pug Dog Club, which had its name changed to the London & Provincial Pug Club in the following year. Both breed clubs flourished for many years with influential people being members of both clubs. They held their annual shows jointly until in 1926 when they merged to form the club we know today as The Pug Dog Club.

Ch. Finsbury Major: The first Champion under the new rules of 1896.

black dog and a black bitch. This happy interlude continued until shows were suspended due to the Great War in 1914. Imagine how upbeat the world of showing must have been in those days for the regular enthusiast. The show circuit included all of the mainland shows, plus the whole of Ireland (there was not yet an Irish Republic). A list of Pug Champions is currently under preparation, but it is difficult to compile and extensive, especially for the blacks.

The first Champion made up in 1896 under the new system was the fawn dog Finsbury Major. He was bred by Mrs C.S. Brittain, and was owned briefly by Mr Willoughby Holdsworth before being sold to Miss Edith Harris of Dublin, who was responsible for making him up. At the end of that year came the first bitch Champion, the outstanding black Chotee, bred by Mr Summers, owned and campaigned by Mrs A. Howard, and then sold on to Mrs S. Trew.

NOVELTY BREEDING

With the dawn of the century and the Edwardian era, the popularity of the Pug declined in favour of Pomeranians and Pekingese. Nevertheless, experimentation was high and we had true-bred white Pugs, which were developed and introduced by Hugh Dalziel. The idea never really caught on and though some shows introduced classes for whites, they soon disappeared.

Next came the long-haired, Pug which also had special classes. This idea lasted a little longer than the whites, but in a short space of time they, too, faded out. One of the best known long-haired Pugs was Hodge.

In 1913 we had the sensational introduction of blue Pugs, developed from black parents by Miss Grace Bellamy. They did breed true in colour, and one specimen was on display at the Natural History Museum until 1979 when it was lost during the move to the new premises in Tring. Although we have a picture of her, sadly it is only in sepia. The timing of such a major development was unfortunate, with war approaching and the decision by the Kennel Club to suspend new registrations during the period of hostilities. It was hard enough for the traditional colours to keep going, so something new had little chance of survival.

BETWEEN THE WARS

If the pre-war period had been prosperous, the post-war period was not. The popularity level of Pugs still lagged behind Pomeranians and Pekingese. Blacks were stripped of their separate status by the Kennel Club. In addition, the Kennel Club no longer allocated CCs to the Pug Dog Club annual show. Times were hard, but Pug breeders are made of stern stuff and the standard was still maintained at a very high level. We also saw the arrival of a new book, *The Pug, its History and Origins* by Mrs Wilhelmine Swainston Goodger, published in 1930. This really did dispel some ancient myths and became the bible for the breed. It is still held in high regard today.

North of the border, the breed fanciers were equally determined; in 1926 they joined forces with the newly merged Pug Dog Club by registering the Scottish Pug Dog Club at the Kennel Club. This club remains with us today despite many trials and tribulations. It goes to show what determination and durability Pugs inspire.

From 1911 to 1913 there was a Northern Pug Club – the

Ch. Chotee: The first bitch Champion.

secretary was J.R. Culshaw – but it ceased to exist due to the First World War. A new attempt to form a club was made in 1928; it was registered as the Northern Pug Dog Club and Mrs Betty Henshall was secretary. The club seems to have been active again post-war, but more of that later.

The bitch I have selected to represent the inter-war period is the black Ch. Miss Penelope. She was bred by Mrs Vincent Curtis in 1922, sired by Massa Sambo of Broadway out of Ch. Penelope. She became the foundation bitch of the Inver kennel run by the Misses Hartrick, Campbell and Morrison. She won six CCs but was better remembered for producing six Champions. In the first litter, when mated to Ch. Dark Dickory, she produced Master Pen of Inver in May 1924. With a repeat mating, she produced Leo of Inver in December 1924. He was passed on to the sire's owner and renamed Dark Dragoon. For the third and fourth litters Dandy Dicker of Baronshalt (son of Dickory) was the sire and in November 1926 she produced Peter and Paul of Inver. In the fourth (and last) litter, July 1927, she produced Penelope's Girl and Penella of Inver. All proved to be very good Champions.

To represent the dogs, Ch. Thundercloud of Swainston has been selected. His record is outstanding considering his career was so severely curtailed by the Second World War. He

was by the black Prempeh of Hopeworth out of Giovanna of Swainston. In 1938, shortly before his first birthday, on the first day of Crufts he was made Best of Breed. On the second day he was made Best Toy Dog at Crufts and won the International Toy Dog Trophy. Later that year, he was Best in Show at the Pug Dog Club show. In 1939 he was again Best of Breed at Crufts and Best in Show at the Pug Dog Club show.

Before war was declared later that year and showing was abruptly halted, he had won five CCs and earned the title Pug of the Century. During this period he was never beaten by another Pug. In the first post-war Pug Dog Club Show in 1946 he finished second to Dark Dan (the first post-war Champion), taking the reserve CC. This was scant consolation, for he had lost his unbeaten record against other Pugs, albeit in his ninth year.

POST-WAR ERA

On a wave of enthusiasm, the Pug Dog Club held two shows in both 1946 and 1947; all four were granted CCs by the Kennel Club. From then until Coronation year in 1953, no more CCs were forthcoming. Fortunately, from that time on, the show has been able to retain Championship status.

Now, however, there were three clubs to wave the flag. The Scottish Pug Dog Club and the Northern Pug Dog Club had

Ch. Thundercloud of Swanston.

joined the fray. From 1955 onwards, regular Open shows were introduced and have since become the norm. Relatively recently members' Limited shows were introduced. This has helped to establish a very stable environment for our breed to flourish. There had also been a distinct rise in breed popularity.

INFLUENTIAL PUGS

From the post-war era to the present day, there have been many high-quality Pugs and so my selection of suitable representatives has not been easy.

Ch. Rosalia of Nanchyl was a fairly obvious choice for the bitches. She was the breed record holder for some time with a total of 37 CCs. She took the record from her great grandmother, Ch. Nanchyl Roxanna (who was awarded 32 CCs). Apart from this impressive record, she was twice Best in Show at General Championship shows.

Her great moment came in 1992 at Crufts. Following in the

POST WAR PUGS

Ch. Rexden Rubstic:
Winner of two
General Championship
Best in Shows.

Ch. Banchory Lace:
One of the
greatest black
Pugs of all time.

footsteps of Thundercloud of Swainston Ch. Cedarwood Blunshill's Nimrod (1967), and Ch. Dingleberry Vega (1977), she won the Toy Group. This time, of course, as a worthy television star.

The choice for the boys was much more difficult. There was a temptation to make it a three-way tie with Ch. Nanchyl Xerxes, Best of Breed at Crufts for three years in succession, against the current breed CC record holder Ch. Hutzpah Harvest Moon of Ansam. Ch. Rexden Rubstic was the third contender, selected. His tally of 27 CCs was not exceptional, but it was his performance against other breeds that sets him apart. On two occasions he was Best in Show at General Championship shows, which must mean that he had that extra little something. Ch. Rosalia of Nanchyl equalled this feat, thus restoring a most wleome parity between the sexes.

To conclude the case for the fawns, we have recent news from Amanda Ellis that the Eastonite kennel has achieved the magic three Champions from one litter. The three fawn Champions are: Eastonite Gill, Eastonite Jak and Eastonite Maureen Myojo. The sire was Northside Paul Eastonite and the dam Mysterious Lady for Joshelle.

To show no bias against blacks, we have included one of perhaps the greatest renown – Ch. Banchory Lace. Owned and bred by Lorna Countess Howe and Miss Lang, she won a total of 27 CCs and was once Best in Show at a General Championship show. All this despite the fact that she contracted hardpad when in her prime. She was nursed back to health and was even able to show again, but not to the same level as before.

THE MODERN ERA

In more recent years, we have been joined by two more breed clubs: the Wales and West of England Club and the West Pennine Club. The first is an established Championship status club and let us hope that the latter follows on shortly. With this new expanded field of activity everything seems set fair for future success. Alas! There is always a snag: in this case, how long can we all afford to travel to show venues with entry costs rising and fuel costs soaring?

At this time, our breed is high in the popularity stakes and recently moved into the top 20 of the 'all breeds' list. There are, however, outside pressures that are growing from the media, the veterinary profession and dog welfare groups, which has been focused against the Kennel Club and some specific breeds. The Pug dog is one of those breeds – if only on the margins.

The Kennel Club is revising Breed Standards of certain breeds, including ours, and, at present, a slightly modified Standard has been agreed by both parties. Pug breeders are

Champion Tidemill Black Yvette: Top Pug Bitch and Top Black Pug 2008. Owned and bred by Terry Purse & Nigel Marsh.
Photo: Alan Walker.

working hard to ensure that they comply, and judges are actively assisting to encourage their efforts. No doubt the new Pug dogs will look more like Pugs of old, as the heavy over-nose wrinkle and tight twisted tail is now frowned upon. We shall see in due course. Breeders have the best interests of the Pug at heart and are determined to produce Pugs to better-than-ever standard, which will be to the benefit of us all.

For more information on the Pug Breed Standard, see Chapter Seven: The Perfect Pug.

THE PUG IN NORTH AMERICA

The USA led the way in the development of the Pug. The first registration of a Pug at the American Kennel Club was in 1885. The first recorded Pug Champion in America was Ch. George, AKC #3286, AKC Stud Pug, 1885. He was born on 1 November 1878, bred by Miss Lelia Tregvan of South Carolina, who imported a bitch in whelp, and George was the result. He was owned by Mrs E.A. Pue of Philadelphia Pa.

Our information implies that Mrs Foster's Banjo was exported around that time, but perhaps a little earlier. His sire was Mrs Monk's Sambo, regarded as one of the five pillars of the Pug breed. He was soon followed by his own son, Champion Bradford Ruby, circa 1885. The next export that we know of was

Master Tragedy, giving direct links back to Click – but neither lived up to expectations.

The American scene is typified by the pedigree of Bob Ivy (see page 30), owned and bred by Dr M.H. Cryer, a prominent Pug personality of the day. The link back to Click and his successors can be seen and there must also have been some early contact with other British breeders not recorded.

Just as it did in the UK, around 1900 the popularity of the Pug plummeted when Pomeranians and Pekingese appeared on the scene. If anything, the decline was greater and longer lasting than that experience here, and from 1900 to 1920 there were very few

The USA has been instrumental in the development of the Pug. This is Am. Ch. Ivanwold Diva at Riversong: Winner of 13 all breed Best in Shows. Bred by Charlotte and Edward Patterson, owned by Carolyn Koch.

Am. Ch. Dhandy's Favorite Woodchuck: Best in Show Westminster 1981, National Specialty winner 1980 and 1981, and winner 56 all breed Best in Shows. Bred by Barbara Braley and Anita Hutchinson.

PEDIGREE OF CH. BOB IVY

Born 23/04/1888. Owner/breeder Dr M.H. Cryer, Philadelphia USA.

Ch. Bob Ivy	Sire: Ch. Dude	Max	Ch. Roderick
			Imp. Dolly
		Imp. Dolly	Toby
			Liz
	Dam: Vestra	Othello	Scamp 11
			Not Known
		Imp. Ruby	Othello
			Not Known

*Toby was (??????) Click out of Hebe.

** Scamp 11 was by Champion Tum Tum 11 out of Belle Petite (Tum Tum tracing back to Click)

Ch. Cameo's Baby Biffle. Winner of the Pug Dog Club of America National Specialty Show in 1992, 1993 and 1994. She was the only bitch in history to win the Show three times. She also won five All-Breed Best in Shows and 9 Specialty Best in Shows. Bred by Joe and Jan Ravotti. Owned by Mrs Alan Robson.

Ch. Ivanwold Senator Sam: Winner of 14 all breed Best in Show, 1980 Toy Group winner, Westminster. Bred by Charlotte and Edward Patterson, owned by Mrs Robert Clarke.

breeders registering Pugs. The first Pug Dog Club of America was founded in 1931 but faded out of existence. A new club was started in 1957, and there are now some 20 Pug Dog Clubs affiliated to the Pug Dog Club of America.

Such is the lack of information that we cannot pick up the story of the Pug in the USA again until the *Pug Dog Club Bulletin* arrived in 1949. Although homespun, this publication contained news of all recent litters and all exports overseas, so we can trace not only the exporters, but also the importers, and find out how their purchases fared.

One of the most prominent exports of this time was Lotus of Longlands who was sold on by Mrs Wyn Lewis. She really did live up to expectation and soon gained her American title as well as producing some fine progeny. This very informative phase continued until 1964 when the new-style bulletin that we have today was introduced. We no longer have this detail.

During this period we had regular communication with some delightful and generous people. There was the round Britain trip in the 1950s by Mrs Elmina Brewster Sewall of the Tarralong kennel and her friend, Miss Harriet Smith. They not only purchased Pugs to take back with them, but left trophies for the clubs. Mrs Brewster Sewall became the first overseas member of the Pug Dog Club. There were many more breed enthusiasts, including Frederick Greenly, Richard Paisley, James Cavallaro and Miss Stegail of the Winna kennel in Canada. In fact, at this time there was a regular round-up of American news and views included in *Dog World* annuals for a number of years but that, too, was discontinued.

THE CURRENT SCENE IN AMERICA

The Pug Dog Club of America now has about 600 members all over the United States and several members from abroad. They hold an annual National Specialty with conformation and all-performance events including obedience, rally and agility. The entry is usually 300-400 Pugs. The club is currently very involved in health issues, such as PDE, hemivertebrae, Legges Perthes disease and others.

The Pug in America has come a long way. Almost every weekend at shows, Pugs are winning in style. Our dogs have become shorter in back, better structured and more balanced than dogs of even 30 years ago. Presentation in the show ring has risen to a fine art. Male exhibitors are in coat and tie, and ladies also 'dress up'.

TOP DOGS
In 1981 Ch. Dhandy's Favorite Woodchuck won Best in Show at the prestigious Westminster Kennel Club. He also won the PDCA National Specialty in 1980 and 1981. He held the record for most All Breed Best in Shows until recently when Ch. Kendoric's Riversong Mulroney won an amazing 65 All Breed Best in Shows. 'Dermot' also won the Toy Group at Westminster in 2006. Truly, Pugs have become a force in the show ring.

Am. Ch. Coral Bay's Superstar, bred by Carol Giles.

INFLUENTIAL BLOODLINES

Certainly the breedings between the Sheffield line and Ch. Wolf's Little Joe was one of the most influential factors for many years. Margery Shriver used Little Joe many times and was very successful. Ch. Broughcastle Balladeer was also a potent sire, producing many Champions, including Ch. Ivanwold Senator Sam and Ch. Ivanwold Pistol Pete, who were multiple Best in Show littermates. Pete produced 36 Champions. Ch. Chalamar's Ancient Dreamer also produced 36 Champions.

LEADING BREEDERS

Some kennels that have contributed to the breed's progress in the past include: Sheffield, Bonjour, Glory, Harper and Fahey.

Am. Ch. Riversong's Broadway Joe: No.1 Pug all systems 2010. Bred and owned by Carolyn Koch.

Current breeders of note include:
- Carol Giles of Coral Bay Pugs
- Joy and Gary Cupp of WooWoo Pugs
- Charlotte Patterson of Ivanwold Pugs
- Carolyn Koch of Riversong Pugs
- Blanche Roberts of Blaque's Pugs
- Doug Huffman of Broughcastle Pugs
- Patt and Ray Kolesar of Tupelo Pugs
- Polly Lamarine of Silvertown Pugs
- Chris Dresser of Dress Circle Pugs.

The Pug in America is in good condition, ever popular and making healthy strides to the future.

A PUG FOR YOUR LIFESTYLE

3

Chapter

The decision to search for that special Pug with whom to share your life surely has to be one of the most important and life-changing moves you will ever make. Owning a dog of any kind should be viewed as a long-term commitment, and owning a Pug is no exception. Your little Pug will, hopefully, be by your side for many years, and from the day he arrives in your home you will be responsible for his day-to-day care and his total well-being. This is a commitment that should not be undertaken lightly and never on impulse.

GIVING TIME

The most valuable thing any dog owner can offer is their time and company, so ask yourself whether you are able to be there for your Pug for the better part of the day, every day, for the foreseeable

future. Many breeders cannot be persuaded to part with a puppy unless they can be assured that someone responsible is to be at home for the majority of the time. There are real reasons for

this. Not unlike a human baby, a young puppy requires an appreciable amount of care and supervision, not to mention the fact that, for the first few weeks at least, he will require feeding

Before you fall in love with a Pug puppy, work out if you have the time and the money to care for him properly.

several times daily. Remember, this puppy has come to you straight from the nest and is accustomed to the company of his siblings, who are also his full-time playmates, so leaving him on his own is just asking for problems to develop.

It is a fact that puppies of this age still require long periods of sleep, but during their waking time they need company to prevent boredom setting in – and the bad habits that are quickly acquired as a direct result of it. House training a puppy successfully is also doomed to failure unless someone is on hand to monitor the little one and is able to act immediately upon his needs. Puppies of this age are unable to wait! It is also worth pointing out that a young Pug who spends long periods of time on his own is never going to develop the full depth of

character and awareness that is the hallmark of so many beloved companion Pugs. For him to realise his true potential and become the dog of your dreams, your little dog will need the stimulation of your company, love and attention.

A prospective Pug owner who works long hours and is away from home on a regular basis should, thus, think very hard indeed and may, rightly, decide to postpone ownership until full commitment can be given. More and more people these days, though, are able to have their dog with them in their workplace, so could this be an option for you? It may be less than ideal for a very young puppy, but for an older, well-behaved dog – providing the environment is both safe and suitable – it can be an ideal solution and work well.

Dog sitting for a friend or even

walking a dog in your spare time for an elderly neighbour can be very fulfilling and might prove to be a compromise that will go at least part way to keeping you involved with the breed until the time is right for you to take on a Pug of your very own.

FINANCIAL COMMITMENT

The financial outlay involved over the coming years should also be thought out, as the cost of looking after a dog properly, plus additional expenses, such as insurance and vet fees, often increase on a yearly basis, even for a fit and healthy dog.

If you prefer to holiday abroad now and then, or want to go away occasionally without your Pug, consider what your options are to ensure his safety and well-being during your absence. The obvious choices are boarding kennels, professional pet sitters or relying on friends and family. You need to be aware of the costs and disruption involved, plus the fact that, whatever you decide, your Pug should only be left with someone in whom you have complete and absolute trust.

WHAT DO YOU WANT FROM YOUR PUG?

You are reading this book, so we can assume you have done some research into the breed, thought the whole thing through, and are now considering that the time could be right to proceed. You have already taken the first steps by thinking that the Pug could well be the one and only dog for you. It's a wise decision, as Pugs

In an ideal world, you would take your Pug on holiday with you.

are very special dogs indeed! Leading on from this, what exactly do you require from your dog? Are you looking simply for companionship or do you want a dog you can compete with in the show ring?

If you require a dog to share and enrich your life, but do not have the slightest desire to show him, your aim is to find a typical, healthy, well-bred and well-reared example of the breed. Your puppy will seem perfect in your eyes, so it is of no consequence if the puppy lacks in some fine detail and so is not quite up to making it big time in the show ring. This alone will make your search much easier and widen your choice.

FINDING A BREEDER

Let us move on now to the search for an approved breeder. This will more than likely commence by approaching one or more of the Pug breed clubs, which are located in various parts of the country. You will find contact details via the internet. The Kennel Club is another likely source or perhaps you are acquainted with someone who owns another breed, who can recommend a responsible Pug breeder. You may be fortunate enough to meet a delightful Pug in your park or on the beach, perhaps, whose owner may be only too happy to talk Pugs with you and point you in the direction of a conscientious breeder.

Perhaps you will hear of a litter bred locally. Puppies born to a charming pet bitch in a suitable home environment can, and often do, turn out extremely well. Bear in mind, though, that the litter is more than likely to have been bred by a novice breeder, which although no bad thing in itself, could mean that the litter

A Pug is a very special dog, but you must decide what you want from him.

You need to find a breeder that has a reputation for producing sound, healthy, typical specimens of the breed.

to an abrupt end the moment the purchase price has been handed over. These litters are rarely reared in ideal conditions; the puppies are often sold at far too young an age, and to anyone who happens to come along, with no attempt to ascertain whether or not the home offered is suitable. The litter may not even have been born on the premises, as puppies are often bought in to sell at a profit. This means the puppy has been exposed to unnecessary health risks and has already experienced the trauma of moving home. Should any problems occur, and this is far more likely in this situation, you can bet your bottom dollar that there will be no response from the seller.

If you do, unwittingly, find yourself in such an establishment and are faced with a mother and undernourished puppy with a staring coat and blown-out tummy, do not fall into the trap of feeling sorry for the puppy and buying him. This will only ensure that the cycle of indiscriminate production will continue.

By the same rule, beware of the breeder who keeps many different breeds, as Pugs do not do well in this kind of situation. The Pug is not considered to be one of the easiest breeds to whelp and rear, and the specialist breeder, who values her good name, will have invested a great deal of time and thought into producing this litter and will, rightly, be very fussy as to where they go. The breeder with the good of the breed at heart will probably have several

has been reared on a learn-as-you-go basis and sired by the nearest available dog with very little thought given as to his suitability for this particular bitch. He may not even have been used at stud before, so it could prove impossible to track his record as a sire; he will more than likely have been selected on his proximity and availability rather than for his bloodlines and temperament.

You will need to ascertain that the litter has been reared correctly and, very importantly, that the puppies are Kennel Club registered. Should this not be the case, ensure that both parents are registered and that you are supplied with the correct

paperwork when collecting the puppy in order that you may register him yourself. This is absolutely essential as, should the puppy turn out well, you may well decide to show him. So, be absolutely sure you have everything in place at the outset, as it could save considerable heartache later on.

Always be wary of anyone who offers you a Pug at considerably less than the going rate, as there is almost always a good reason for his. Never consider buying a puppy from a puppy farm, where litters are produced indiscriminately. The price and instant availability may be tempting, but you can bet that all interest in the puppy will come

40

Whether you choose a male (right) or a female (left) comes down to personal preference.

years of experience in caring for Pugs of all ages, and be willing to be a source of a lifetime support and advice. For the first time owner, taking home a very small Pug baby, it can be invaluable to know there is someone capable of supporting you, who is just a phone call away. A responsible breeder may also offer to be involved in rehoming your Pug should your circumstances change.

Expect to be asked detailed questions about your home and your family set-up. The breeder may want to know of other family members, including other pets, and about your lifestyle. A breeder who is willing to hand over a puppy at a motorway service station to someone they have never met and know little about should be given a wide berth. The same applies to anyone who breeds purely and simply for financial gain; these are the people who will cut corners in order to maximise profit. You may well have to travel some distance to find the right breeder, but this could prove to be more than worth the effort involved.

MALE OR FEMALE?

The next decision you have to make is whether you want a male (dog) or female (bitch). If your inclinations lean towards a bitch but you feel you cannot cope with seasons and plan to have her spayed at the earliest opportunity, then do please consider having a dog instead. Unlike some other breeds, there is very little difference between the sexes in Pugs. On the whole, people tend to think bitches are more faithful and easier to handle, but this is not the case. Dogs can and do make equally wonderful companions.

Neutering a bitch, although accepted by most vets now as a routine operation, still constitutes major surgery and anaesthetic always carries some risk. In contrast, the operation to castrate a dog is relatively simple, although it should only be done if found to be necessary, and only when the dog has attained physical maturity.

COLOUR

Before you visit a litter, you will probably have decided if your preference is for a fawn or a black puppy, as many breeders may only keep one colour. However, you will usually find that someone who keeps only fawns, for example, will be more than happy to put you in touch with a reliable breeder who has blacks. Pug people, almost without exception, are most helpful and friendly.

If you cannot make up your mind as to colour, get in touch with a breeder who has both colours so that you may see fawn and black Pugs together.

VISITING THE LITTER

The breeder you eventually decide upon will probably invite you to visit when the puppies are around six weeks of age. It is most beneficial to see them at this time, although you must bear in mind that it is essential the babies stay where they are for another few weeks at the very least. A caring breeder could well ask if she can visit your home to see where the puppy will spend his life and to ensure that everything is fine and dandy before handing him over.

Try not to be in too much of a hurry and remember the old adage that good things are worth waiting for. This is very true in this case, as you may well have to be prepared to wait a while for a suitable puppy; a successful and experienced breeder will be more

than likely to have a list of would-be owners in waiting.

Do not be afraid to ask questions about the puppies' background. A caring breeder should be more than willing to talk about their stock, and you may also wish to enquire about how and where the litter has been reared. For example:

- Do you consider it a suitable environment?
- Have the puppies had enough space and freedom to develop and play?
- Do they appear well cared for – i.e. well fed, warm and clean?
- Have they been sympathetically handled from birth and well socialised so that they are used to normal household noise?
- Has the rearing been trouble-free?
- Have any close relatives, especially the parents, had any serious health problems?
- Have the parents had any breed-specific health checks?
- How many puppies were born in the litter?
- Will you have a choice of puppy?

In this day and age, we have all become accustomed to being offered options in most things, but do not be put off if you cannot pick from the litter. Pug litters are relatively small compared to some breeds and, more often than not, the dedicated breeder will have bred the litter in order to keep a puppy to carry on the line. It should be possible to see the

The puppies should be reared in a clean, hygienic environment with plenty of space to play.

mother with the babies, except perhaps in very exceptional circumstances. Ideally, you will also be able to see other close family members, perhaps an older sibling who has been retained from a previous litter, or a grandmother or aunt of the puppies. This will give you some idea of how your puppy will look when mature.

The fact that the sire of the puppies does not live on the premises is not something to worry about; the breeder will, more than likely, be able to furnish you with some of his history and background and maybe a photograph of him. Many serious breeders do not keep a stud dog of their own, preferring instead to use the services of a really first-class dog who has been shown, and has notched up some creditable wins under experienced judges and in good company. He may well be the sire of several promising litters with winning progeny already in the show ring.

A COMPANION PUG

If you are looking for a Pug purely and simply as a companion and have no intention of taking up showing, then I would suggest you search out a calm and contented Pug mother who is typical of her breed. When you visit the litter, do, please, be prepared for the fact that the dam of the babies will most decidedly not be at her best at this time. In actual fact, she is more than likely going to be looking at her very worst, and

It is important to see the mother with her pups as this will give you some idea of how the puppies may turn out.

particularly so if she has done a brilliant job and has several thriving offspring. Many Pug mothers look a little on the skinny side when the babes have been finally weaned, and almost always proceed to cast every hair just about the time the puppies are ready to fly the nest!

Look carefully at this family. Their mother may be finding them a little tiresome and demanding by now, but she will still wish to be with them from time to time and it is good to see them together. Cast your eye away from the weakest, skinniest puppy (if there is one) who may be hanging around in the background with his tail down.

He may well deserve the sympathy vote, but you are far better advised, as a new Pug owner, to focus your attention instead on the playful little smarty-pants guy who is gazing up at you longingly and waiting, somewhat impatiently, for you to notice him! This little fellow is probably nicely rounded, firm on his legs and, most importantly in a pet dog, both curious and responsive.

A SHOW PUPPY

Choosing a puppy to show can be extremely difficult and is by no means an exact science. Puppies, like most young animals, tend to have growth

THE SHOW PUPPY

The breeder will 'stand' a puppy which will help you assess conformation.

spurts at different ages and can alter out of all recognition in a short space of time, so even experienced breed specialists can often get it wrong.

The beauty of a dog is very much in the eye of the beholder; the fact is that different dogs will win from show to show under experienced judges, and even a Champion Pug with many wins under his belt cannot be expected to win top honours every time he goes out. Although all judges must judge against a Breed Standard issued by the Kennel Club, it still remains a very personal approach. If judges were permitted no personal preferences, dog shows and all the resulting pleasure would cease to exist – the whole thing could boringly and predictably be done by computer. Another

show, a different judge and the results can be very different, too, although it must be said that a first-class dog who conforms correctly to the Breed Standard can always expect to finish somewhere near the head of the line.

If you are not sufficiently confident to know what you are looking for, and few prospective owners are, then ask someone who has proven experience to advise you. Alternatively, put your faith in the breeder, who, if you have chosen correctly, will be willing to point out the faults and virtues of each puppy. Few successful breeders will wish to see a puppy they have bred shown at a high level of competition if he does not come up to scratch. The end decision, most surely, has to be yours, but

do always bear in mind that however carefully the litter has been planned and reared, there can never be any worthwhile guarantees when buying a young puppy to show. All that can ever be said, with any degree of truth and honesty, is that the baby is well bred, responsibly reared and considered at the time of sale to be very promising.

The period between taking home the young puppy and introducing him to the show ring at maybe six months of age can be a crucial one, as puppies can and do alter considerably during this vital growth time. Allowing that the little one has received the best start in life, whether or not he develops his true potential is pretty much down to you from now on. It is therefore vital that you do your utmost to

The head should be well-shaped with some promise of wrinkle.

The limbs should be sturdy and well boned.

A positive, out-going temperament is a top priority in a potential show dog.

get it right and, above all, follow the breeder's advice, only making changes very gradually. Given everything is done as prescribed, there will still be many a promising puppy who ends up as a mediocre adult and vice versa. That is the name of the game and is all part and parcel of the appeal and excitement of breeding.

ASSESSING A LITTER

On your first and any subsequent visit to the breeder's establishment, spend as long as you can sitting comfortably somewhere a little out of the way, where you can look at the litter being carefree in their own little world, sublimely oblivious of what the future holds for them. Have patience and wait until the puppies have forgotten about you and are totally relaxed, because this is when you will see them as they really are.

We will take it for granted that the litter has a good genetic background and has been given a good start in life – so what do you look for when seeking a puppy of this age with show potential? Opinions will vary, but I would suggest to look first for good general conformation and temperament. Some puppies will be pushy, and others more retiring, so watch them playing to get some idea of their character.

A Pug baby coming up to the 8- to 10-week mark should be a well-balanced, outgoing puppy and feel heavier than he looks when you pick him up, as the Breed Standard calls for the adult to be "multum in parvo". Roughly translated, this means "a lot in a little", so we are looking for a compact but strong little dog. Look for the following features:

- The basic beginnings of a well-shaped head with a wide underjaw. This will be necessary to provide support and shape for the whole face.
- The promise of some wrinkle on the head.
- A kind, dark eye.
- Straight front legs, nicely rounded ribs, a level topline and well-placed shoulders.
- A broad chest, important for heart room.
- Sturdy, well-boned limbs.
- A high-set tail already carried well over his back and attempting to curl.
- Jet-black pigmentation, the darker the better, with good definition between the colours

45

on the fawns, although this is something that can improve with age.

- A dense black colour with the much-desired single coat is the ideal in a black, who should have no patches of white hair.

Never choose a puppy with an obvious and glaring constructional fault, such as bowed front legs, poor shoulder placement, untypical head or low-set tail, hoping that time may correct the fault – because it will not. You do need to be aware, though, that the young puppy cannot be expected to display the finish of the adult, in particular with regard to head qualities.

Look for a puppy who is short-coupled – this being the length of body between the point that can be felt at the end of the ribs to the hindquarters. There are two kinds of ear in Pugs: the rose, which is usually very fine and therefore folds over and back, and the button, where the ear flap folds forward. Either is acceptable, although some judges may favour a small, neat, button ear, given that all else is equal. Puppies going through the teething stages often fly their ears, meaning the ears are not held neatly in the adult position but rather spring out from the head, as in wings! This will almost always settle down when teething is finished. The tail also is often affected by teething troubles, so this is something to bear in mind.

An older puppy of 12-plus weeks is more than likely to appear to be all arms and legs, but these are stages that most normal puppies go through. It is probably in your best interests to be guided by the breeder here, who will know what is to be expected at that particular age. A minor cosmetic fault is something you may have to settle for and if only a small glitch, may well improve with age. The prospective exhibitor should always keep in the front of his mind that the perfect dog has yet to be bred so, please, never set your heart on utter perfection. Decide what are your priorities, as you may well have to reach an acceptable compromise on some detail or other. Be prepared for this and do not set your sights unrealistically high.

Correct soundness, type and temperament are vital for both a pet and a show dog, so these should be considered an absolute essential for any prospective owner, whether or not he aspires to showing. To advise someone

COLLECTING YOUR PUPPY

The age at which the breeder is willing to hand over the puppy will vary considerably from breeder to breeder. Present-day thinking by many vets and dog people is that the optimum time for the puppy to make the changeover smoothly, and begin life in his forever home, is just over eight weeks of age. Other people disagree with this, and it is not unusual to meet a breeder who feels it is beneficial to the long-term interest of the puppy to keep the litter together in their birthplace for several weeks longer. Pug puppies are quite small in comparison to some breeds and can be very vulnerable when they first arrive in a new and busy home situation. Individuals must decide for themselves which is the better route to go down; if the prospective owner and breeder have different views on this then surely a compromise can be reached.

how to check for soundness is almost impossible to project in print, but a rough guide may be as follows: a puppy of six weeks or so may still be a shade wobbly and unsure on his legs, but at 8-10 weeks he should be moving around confidently without undue effort or puffing and panting, and, above all, looking at ease when he does so. Construction plays an enormous part in soundness. If a Pug is put together well, he will, 99 times out of 100, move soundly.

A positive temperament is as vital in a show dog as in a pet – maybe even more so, as the show dog has to learn to cope calmly with being handled by different people and often in strange places. He also needs the spirit to make the most of himself, so thus needs some inborn bounce and self-esteem. A timid puppy may well improve in confidence, but this should never be taken for granted and could well lead to considerable disappointment. A 'typy', well-constructed Pug that is also shy and withdrawn is unlikely ever to hit the top spots. It is the dog that enjoys every minute of being in the ring that is best equipped to catch the judge's eye.

Instinct can play a big part in selecting a puppy – just be relaxed and you will, more than likely, find that you are drawn to one particular pup. Should this be the case, then focus your attention on that puppy, as the chances are that he has decided for you and will become the chosen one who will accompany you home.

TAKING ON AN OLDER DOG

An adult Pug can actually prove to be a far wiser choice for perhaps an older person, or someone who feels unable to deal with the physical demands of a young puppy while still being perfectly capable of taking on and caring for the needs of a mature dog. When considering adopting an older dog, do remember that you are proposing to take on the finished Pug who has been brought up and become accustomed to someone else's ways and routine. He will need time and understanding, not to mention unlimited patience and perseverance, in order to reshape and adapt himself to your lifestyle. This, given your input, he will surely manage, and once a real relationship between you has been established, he will repay you most handsomely in terms of loyalty and devotion.

When looking for an older dog, it is worth approaching a breeder, as they are often limited as to the number of adults they can keep and may well be able to help. A breeder may prefer to rehome an older bitch, for example, who still has much to offer and will benefit from spending her remaining years as a much-loved pet. She has perhaps bred and reared a

It may suit your lifestyle to miss out on the puppy stage and take on an older dog.

couple of litters, but still has many years ahead to look forward to.

Alternatively, you may be offered a youngish dog, who has perhaps been run on to show, but, due to some minor fault or other, has failed to make the grade. This should not in any way affect his ability to make a perfect companion dog.

Most of these dogs will settle easily in a loving pet home and quickly adapt and enjoy the one-to-one attention. It is well worth enquiring if they have been properly house trained, though, as it requires time and patience to train a dog who is well past the puppy stage. If you are such a person, however, and prepared to persevere and cope smilingly with the odd accident, it is perfectly possible to house train even a much older dog.

RESCUED DOGS

Adopting a rescued dog calls for both time and patience, as most reputable rescue organisations try to match the dog with the home and therefore their waiting lists are not dealt with on the usual 'first come, first served' basis. This could well mean a considerable wait for a dog to turn up who is, hopefully, going to be the right dog for you. Looking on the bright side, it may also mean he could be there already and waiting for you to collect him!

Be honest and forthcoming when you are asked a

Pugs of all ages can be successfully rehomed.

comprehensive list of questions, because any organisation that does not require this is not worth their salt. It goes without saying that it is in the dog's best interest for you to disclose as much information as is possible about yourself and the way you live. You do need to be prepared for the fact that very little may be known about the dog you are offered.

Dogs come into rescue for many and varied reasons. Sometimes a full history is known, but sometimes absolutely nothing, not even, sadly, the dog's previous name. Remember also that there are rescued dogs who may have suffered neglect or even ill-treatment over a period of

time, and you will need to take on board how this may affect him. This may not have been deliberate; it could have been down to the inability of the previous owner to cope, or even innocent ignorance of the dog's requirements. Most usually, Pugs come into rescue due to a change in the owner's circumstances or the ill-health or death of the former owner. It is rarely through any fault or shortcomings of their own.

Most breed clubs have a number of caring and dedicated people who devote much of their time and effort into taking in and rehoming rescued dogs, so this is likely to be your first and best line of enquiry.

THE RIGHT MATCH

Pugs of all ages, including really golden oldies, have been rehomed successfully and can prove most rewarding, given that the right home is found and the changeover is made as smoothly as possible. Do realise that for at least the first few weeks, the Pug will not be confident enough to display his real temperament so this may not be truly apparent until he has his feet well under the table, so to speak! Are you attracted to the Pug offered? Does he like you and is there at least some degree of initial rapport? When adopting a dog that has been previously owned, you are highly unlikely to be offered a selection, so if you are able to go with an open mind and are not too set on a particular age, sex or colour, you are far more likely to be suited within a reasonable time limit. In short, the more flexible you are, the easier it will be.

Spend as much time as is possible with the Pug before deciding whether or not to take him home, and feel free to ask questions about what is known of his previous life, as this could be vital in helping you to settle him in and making him feel secure. Where, for example, did he sleep in his previous home? Is he accustomed to being left for short periods now and then? What, if anything, is known of his feeding regime? The little things that seem almost too trivial to mention can, in fact, be of great importance to the dog and any small detail that may be passed on about his former routine could prove invaluable.

Bear in mind that, for the Pug himself, just the fact of having to change homes is a traumatic experience, which is bound to affect him. It will take time and love for a bond to be forged between you, so do not expect it to happen

overnight. The world he knew and understood has gone forever, and he will need considerable tender, loving care and understanding to enable him to cope with his new, unexpected change of life.

SUMMING UP

Pugs are delightful and extremely amenable and adaptable little dogs, who are full of character and, on the whole, are extremely pleasant and easy to live with. They are truly gregarious, being one of the few breeds I know of who really love and relish the company of their own kind. Their requirements are straightforward and simple – all a Pug asks is that his needs are met by the person who loves him and that he can share time with that person as much as is possible. In return, he

will give you a lifetime of whole-hearted devotion, the like of which, I promise, you could never imagine.

More than any other breed of dog of which I have experience, the Pug has an inherent desire to please his owner. Once someone has fallen for the breed, they rarely desert it for another. My only word of warning is to say that most Pug people will agree that owning a Pug can become somewhat addictive. So, when acquiring one of these magical little charmers for the first time, do, please, be prepared: the great majority of breeders and exhibitors, including the writer and most of her friends, began by buying one little Pug, purely as a pet!

Which is where, I believe, we came in...

Watch out – owning Pugs can be addictive....

THE NEW ARRIVAL

While you are waiting to collect your Pug puppy, you can spend the time getting your home and garden ready for the new arrival. Your pup will probably be aged between 9 and 12 weeks, so he will be small and vulnerable – but also full of lively curiosity. It is important to invest the time in making your home as safe and secure as possible.

GARDEN SAFETY

The garden is full of hazards for a Pug, who will want to explore every nook and cranny. The first job is to check the fencing. Some Pugs will go round trying to find a small hole or gap to escape, while others will never bother. However, it is better to be safe than sorry. You will also need to check that gates can be securely fastened.

There are some plants or bushes in the garden, such as roses or shrubs with prickles, which could prove hazardous. The curious Pug will want to investigate and because his eyes protrude, they are especially vulnerable. It is not uncommon for the eyeball to be scratched, resulting in an ulcer.

There are also a number of plants and shrubs that are toxic to dogs, so you will need to check this out. You can find out more by researching on the internet, or you can ask from advice from a garden centre.

Garden chemicals, such as insecticides and weedkillers, pose great danger. They are highly toxic and should be avoided at all costs. You must also ensure that your garden shed is securely locked so your Pug cannot gain entry at any time.

A puppy has no sense of danger so you need to make your home and garden 100 per cent safe and secure.

POISONOUS PLANTS

The following list is not complete, but serves as a useful guide.

HOUSE PLANTS
Castor Bean
Daffodil
Dieffenbachia (Dumb Cane)
Elephant Ear
Hyacinth
Narcissus
Oleander
Rosary Pea

PLANTS IN FLOWER GARDENS
Autumn Crocus
Bleeding Heart
Foxglove

Iris
Larkspur
Lily-of-the-Valley
Monkshood

PLANTS IN FIELDS
Buttercups
Jimson Weed (Thorn Apple)
Nightshade
Poison Hemlock
Star of Bethlehem

TREES AND SHRUBS
Black Locust

Elderberry
Oak trees
Wild and cultivated cherries

ORNAMENTAL PLANTS
Azaleas
Daphne
Golden Chain
Jasmine
Lantana Camara (Red Sage)
Laurels
Rhododendrons
Wisteria
Yew

If you have a swimming pool, this should be fenced so it does not form part of your Pug's territory. A swimming pool is even more dangerous than a pond, because if a dog falls in, he has no way of getting out. Ideally a garden pond should also be fenced.

It is a good idea to allocate a toilet area for your Pug to use. This is helpful when you are training him to spend outside, as he associates the place with what he is required to do. It also makes cleaning up a simple procedure.

PREPARING YOUR HOME

If you have not had a dog before, or if it has been a long time since you had a puppy in your home, you need to make a thorough evaluation of potential troublespots. A puppy is bound to get up to mischief – and it is impossible to supervise him every second. The most obvious danger comes from trailing electric wires. These can be easy to reach and, as far as your puppy is concerned, they appear tempting to chew. Obviously, the consequences could be lethal, so make sure that all wires are

secured well out of reach.

Curtains and soft furnishings may be seen as an attraction. The best plan is to prohibit your puppy from going into rooms where he could do damage, or make sure he is only allowed entry when you are there to supervise. The same applies to ornaments – if your puppy can reach them, they are not safe – and neither is your puppy. In the kitchen, check the fastenings on all cupboards that are at ground level. This applies particularly to the cupboard where you keep cleaning agents and other chemicals that could prove harmful.

BUYING EQUIPMENT

To begin with, your Pug will not need very much equipment, but there are a few items that it is worth buying before your new puppy arrives home.

PLAYPEN

A playpen is an invaluable item of equipment, and will certainly make the next few months a lot less stressful. A puppy who is used to going in a playpen will feel secure in his own cosy den. You can equip it with a bed and some toys so he has a place to rest and to play. It can be used at times when you cannot supervise him during the day, and he can also sleep in it at night. It will also be an aid to cleanliness, as the pen can have paper on the floor in the front half so that the puppy will associate paper with toilet training.

If you buy a wire pen, make sure it is made up of small squares so that your puppy cannot get his feet and legs through the gaps. If there are big gaps a puppy will jump up; one of his front legs could slip through, and he may damage a shoulder.

The playpen should be located in a warm, draught-free area. Many Pug owners opt for the kitchen, if there is enough room to position it in a safe place. This allows your puppy to be involved in family life, but he is out of harm's way. This is

A play pen can be kitted out so your puppy has the perfect place to rest and play.

particularly important with a small puppy that can get underfoot.

CRATE/CARRIER

In addition to a playpen, you should also invest in a small crate or a carrier. This can be used as a safe means of transporting your Pug in the car, as long as the crate or carrier is firmly secured. If you are travelling away from home and

cannot take your playpen, the crate or carrier can be used for overnight accommodation. This is particularly important if you are staying in a 'dog-friendly' hotel or holiday cottage, and you want to be 100 per cent confident that your Pug does not do any damage.

BED

A soft, cosy bed is needed so that your puppy can feel warm

Your puppy will appreciate some warm, cosy bedding.

You will find out whether a lead or a harness will suit your Pug as he grows older.

and comfortable. It is not recommended to get a basket, as Pugs are inclined to chew the edges and so expose sharp ends of the basketwork. This could be hazardous; puppies have been known to damage their eyes on the sharp edges. There is a wide range of beds to choose from – but it may be best to wait until your puppy is beyond the chewing phase before making a major investment.

BEDDING

The best type of bedding to buy is synthetic fleece. This is machine-washable and is easy to dry so you can make sure that your Pug's bed is clean and hygienic at all times. This type of bedding is available from most pet stores; you will need at least two pieces so you can replace the bedding when it needs washing.

STAIRGATE

A Pug puppy should not be allowed to go up and down the stairs, as each time he jumps down, he will jar his shoulders, and muscles and ligaments can be damaged, causing lameness. This means the puppy has to be rested to allow for healing, which is very problematic when you have a young puppy that is bursting with energy. The best plan is to invest in a stairgate so your puppy cannot venture upstairs. You may also find it useful to buy an additional gate if you want to exclude your puppy from certain rooms, such as the sitting room, at times when you cannot supervise him.

BOWLS

Another important item for your puppy is a feeding bowl. Saucers are not good, as puppies lick the food off the edges and on to the floor. The best type is made of stainless-steel with an upright rim so the puppy can get his feet right up to the dish. This makes it easier on the shoulders, as the pup can get at the food without straining. The advantage of this type of bowl is that it is virtually indestructible and is easy to keep clean.

Your Pug will also need a bowl for water, which should be freely available at all times. Some owners opt for a ceramic bowl, which is heavy and cannot be tipped over. However, this type of bowl is breakable, so you might prefer to buy a second stainless-steel bowl and use it for water.

COLLAR AND LEAD

Your Pug puppy will not be able to go out for walks until he is fully vaccinated, but he can get used to wearing a collar as soon as he arrives home. You can also practise lead walking in the garden.

The collar you buy should be narrow; wide collars do not suit Pug necks. The collar should be tight enough so as not to be able to get it over the head without undoing it. You may need to start with a baby collar and buy a bigger one when your Pug is fully grown.

The type of lead you buy is a matter of personal preference, as long as it has a secure trigger fastening. Some people prefer to use a harness, but start with a lead and see how your Pug progresses.

For advice on lead training, see Chapter Six: Training and Socialisation.

GROOMING GEAR

The Pug has a low-maintenance coat, so you will not have to buy a lot of grooming equipment. The minimum you will need is:

- A stiff-bristled brush for general adult grooming.
- A soft brush for puppy grooming.
- A fine-toothed comb for removing the soft, fluffy undercoat when it is shedding.

TOYS

Puppies love to have toys – most prefer soft toys to chase after and then pounce on for a good shake. Beware of anything that can be removed from a toy, such as eyes or squeakers that could be swallowed. Some Pugs will go to sleep sucking a soft toy or knead it with their feet as though they were feeding from their mother. It is not only puppies that love soft toys: adult Pugs will also play with them. If your dog has toys of his own, there is a better chance that he will not damage things that he is not allowed.

Pug puppies love to play and will enjoy a variety of toys.

- Nail-clippers.
- Toothbrush and toothpaste.

For advice on grooming, see Chapter Five: The Best of Care.

ID

When your Pug puppy has finished his course of inoculations and is ready to go out and about, he should wear a collar with ID attached. The best type of ID is an engraved disc, with your name, address and telephone number. Do not include your Pug's name, as this could be counterproductive if anyone ever attempted to steal him. Remember to check the disc on a regular basis, as it can become scratched or rubbed, and if your Pug likes to go exploring in undergrowth, it could become detached.

You should also consider getting a form of permanent ID. This could take the form of a tattoo, but most owners opt for microchipping. This is a simple procedure, performed by a vet, who inserts a tiny microchip beneath the skin. This carries your contact details, which can be detected by a scanner.

FINDING A VET

In some cases, the breeder will have started your puppy's vaccination programme, depending on the age of the puppy. Even if this is the case, your pup will still need a second vaccination within two weeks, so it is important to register with a vet before you collect him. Ideally, you want to find a vet who is used to treating Pugs; if the breeder lives locally, you can ask for a recommendation. As a breed, Pugs do not have major health issues, but if an anaesthetic is ever needed – which is more likely in older Pugs – it must be very carefully administered. The Pug is a brachycephalic breed, and is therefore vulnerable to respiratory problems in this situation. If too much anaesthesia is given, it can end in tragedy.

Before you register, visit the practice to find out what services are available, and how emergency cover is provided. This will also give you the opportunity to talk to the staff, so you can gauge if it is the type of place where your Pug is likely to receive the best care and attention.

ARRIVING HOME

Ideally, you will have arranged to collect your Pug in the morning so he has the rest of the day to settle into his new home. This can be a very daunting experience for a puppy, so try not to overwhelm him with too much fuss and attention.

It is a legal requirement for your dog to have some form of ID when he is public places.

COLLECTING YOUR PUPPY

At last it is time to collect your puppy. Despite all the excitement, it is important to check that you are given all the relevant paperwork. This usually includes:

- A three-generation pedigree
- A transfer form from the Kennel Club, which will enable you to transfer the puppy to your ownership.
- Insurance cover for six weeks from the date of getting the puppy.
- If the puppy has been vaccinated, you should be given his vaccination card.
- Details of worming and when the next treatment is due.
- Diet sheet, detailing the type of food and the quantity that should be fed as your puppy grows up.
- Contract of sale.

In addition, the breeder will probably give you a sample of food to last for the first few days. This is to avoid the risk of stomach upset, which could easily happen if a puppy has a sudden change of diet.

After weeks of careful rearing, it is time for the puppies to go to their new homes.

Start by taking him into the garden and allowing him to explore. Take him to his toilet area, and, if he performs, give him lots of praise. Next take him into the house and show him his playpen. Encourage him to go inside and explore by using a treat or a toy.

MEETING THE FAMILY

It is very tempting to ask friends and neighbours to come and meet the new arrival – but this would not be very fair on your puppy. He needs to meet his family first and get to know them before he widens his circle of acquaintance.

Pug puppies are very good with children, but all interactions should be carefully supervised. Children should not be allowed to pick up the puppy, as a Pug pup has very strong shoulders and can really fight to be put down. If you are not aware of this, the puppy can easily be dropped and be quite badly injured. It is better for children to sit on the floor and play with the puppy with a suitable toy.

MOUTHING

I have never known of an aggressive Pug puppy, but some can bite when they play. This is natural behaviour between littermates, but your puppy needs to learn that this is not acceptable when interacting with people. You can teach him to inhibit mouthing behaviour in the following way:

- Get a small treat and show it to your puppy. Then close your fist around the treat.
- Your puppy will try to get the treat by mouthing your hand. The instant he does this, give a sharp yelp – and withdraw your hand. A pup knows he has gone too far with his littermates if they give a yelp of pain, or his mother may give a warning growl. You are reproducing this

reaction, which tells your pup to cease the behaviour.

- Now offer the treat again, and repeat the scenario above if your pup tries to mouth you. He will soon learn this strategy is not working and will probably wait for a split second while he decides what he should do.
- At this instant, offer him the treat and give him lots of praise.

Repeat this at frequent intervals and your puppy will soon learn that if he waits quietly and does not mouth you, he gets a treat. You can also introduce the cue "Gently" when he is taking the treat nicely.

OTHER PETS

If you already have a dog at home, you will want to make sure that relations with the new puppy get off to a good start. Start by introducing them in the

garden where the resident dog will feel more relaxed. You may want to keep the resident dog on the lead for the initial introduction, just to ensure he is not too rough. But it is advisable to let him off the lead as soon as possible so that he is free to greet the youngster. Both dogs will read each other's body language, and, in most cases, a puppy will show he is subservient to the resident dog. Allow the two dogs to get to know each other without interference, and they will soon accept each other.

It is understandable if the resident dog feels a bit put out to begin with, so make sure you give him lots of attention so he does not become jealous. Your puppy will not be able to go out for walks in the first few weeks, so you can make this a special time for the resident dog. Usually, friction between two dogs is caused by jealousy, so make sure you do not fall into this trap.

In time, a Pug will learn to live in harmony with the family cat.

Cats are good at taking care of themselves, so as long as your cat has a high surface to escape to, he has nothing to fear from an inquisitive puppy. You will need to supervise early interactions, just in case your puppy becomes too boisterous and the cat decides to strike with her claws. Again, a Pug's eyes can be particularly vulnerable in this situation.

FEEDING YOUR PUPPY

When your puppy first arrives in his new home, he will need three meals per day. Hopefully, the breeder will have given you enough food to last for the first few days, so your puppy will not have to change diet. It may well be that your puppy is reluctant to eat to begin with. He has so much to get used to, he is simply too unsettled to eat all his food. If this happens, give him 10 minutes to see if he will eat any more, and then take up the bowl and give him fresh food at his next mealtime. In a couple of days, he will be clearing the bowl in record time. However, if you do have any concerns, contact your vet.

For more information on diet and nutrition, see Chapter Five: The Best of Care.

THE FIRST NIGHT

This is a tough time for a puppy; he has left his mother and littermates, and everything that is familiar to him. Instead of snuggling down for the night in a nest of warm puppies, he has

It is hard for a puppy to settle at night without the comfort and warmth of his littermates.

to cope on his own. In this situation, you must start as you mean to go on. It is inevitable that your puppy will cry, but if you go rushing to him, he will quickly learn that if he cries, you come running.

If you want to train your puppy to be independent, it is best to ignore his cries. This may seem hard-hearted, but if you have left him safe in his playpen, with warm bedding, you know he will come to no harm. It may help if you leave him with a soft toy to cuddle up to, and, if it is cold, a hot-water bottle, making

sure it is in a secure cover.

In time, your puppy will settle, and when you come down the next morning, he will be delighted to see you. After a few nights, he will understand the night-time routine and will settle as soon as you put him to bed.

HOUSE TRAINING

House training is a top priority, and you can start as soon as your puppy arrives in his new home. Take him out to explore the garden and give him lots of praise if he relieves himself.

You will need to take your puppy out at the following times:

- When he first wakes in the morning
- After meals
- After play sessions
- When he wakes up from a nap
- Last thing at night.

You should take your puppy out at least every two hours during the course of the day. If you stick to this regime, your puppy will soon realise that he has to be clean in the house. A pup will usually indicate that he needs to go out. Some will cry to go out, others will become agitated and unsettled. A sure sign that a puppy needs to go out is if you see him circling as he tries to find the right spot. In this instance, pick him up and take him outside without delay.

Most breeders will train puppies to relieve themselves on paper. The pen will be lined with paper, and the puppies learn to associate paper with relieving themselves. Paper can be placed near the door that leads outside, and the pup will use this if no one is available to let him out. However, the best plan is to be available to supervise your puppy's trips out to the garden, so you can be on hand to praise him when he performs.

Some people say that Pugs are not clean dogs, but I have found that most will quickly become used to going outside and do not like soiling their pens or beds.

HANDLING

It is important that your Pug gets used to being handled so that he is happy to accept grooming and routine care procedures. It will also mean that he will tolerate being examined by a vet.

Start by standing your puppy on a table. This will give you more control, and your pup will learn that this is where he goes when he is being groomed. If you plan to show your puppy, you can teach him to stand correctly, making sure you reward him when he is still and quiet.

BRUSHING

Initially, use a soft brush on the coat, just so your puppy gets used to the sensation of being groomed. Be firm if he tries to wriggle, and give lots of praise

Vigilance is the key to successful house training.

HANDLING

A puppy needs to get used to being handled from an early age.

Be gentle as you check the teeth and gums.

A quick wipe with a moist tissue will keep a pup clean and fresh.

when he co-operates. Do not expect your pup to stay still for too long – just a couple of minutes will do to begin with – and reward him when you have finished grooming.

NAILS

A Pug puppy's nails can get very pointed and sharp, so they will need to be trimmed on a regular basis. You will also need to keep the dewclaws, which are the equivalent of thumbs, trimmed short if they have not been removed. This is important, as if a Pug gets any irritation in the eye, the first thing he does is rub it with his paw and the dewclaw can scratch the eye. For the first few weeks you can use scissors to trim the nails. After that, they become too strong, and you will need to use nail-clippers.

HOUSE RULES

Deciding what is allowed – and what is not allowed – is a matter of personal choice, but there are a few points worth bearing in mind. It is inadvisable to let a puppy get up on the furniture, as he is liable to jump off on his own and can very easily damage his shoulders and legs. If you allow him on the sofa for a cuddle, make sure you invite him, and afterwards place him back on the floor.

If the puppy is to be a family pet, you can teach him basic obedience commands, which will mean that you have a calm, well-behaved companion. If you have guests, it can be useful to be able to put your Pug away for the duration, as not everyone is dog-minded. Your puppy therefore needs to learn to stay

on his own for short periods. He may cry to begin with, but this should be ignored or he will persist in the hope of getting his own way.

Some Pugs have been trained in obedience and have done very well, but others are not very obedient at all – Pugs seem to be able to ignore you completely if they feel like it. However, it is important that your Pug understands his place in the family and is willing to co-operate with you. *For information on training, see Chapter Six.*

EXERCISE

Initially, your Pug puppy will get as much exercise as he needs from playing in the garden. You can then graduate to going for short walks so that he gets used to walking by your

Teach your puppy to accept spending some time on his own.

circulation. If a Pug is sitting on a seat and the car has to stop suddenly, he can be badly injured. A dog guard between the back seats and the estate part or the hatchback area of your car means the Pug can be free, but beware of opening the back hatch, as he can suddenly dart out. Remember, even a Pug puppy can run very fast.

Never leave your Pug in a car when it is sunny – even with the windows open – as it will get far too hot and the dog will soon be in great distress. This is true of all breeds, but particularly the short-muzzled Pug. Nowadays it is much easier travelling with your Pug, as most cars have air conditioning so the car can be kept really cool. This makes it far more restful for both Pug and owners, as the dogs will not pant and so will often sleep on the journey.

REHOMING A PUG

If you have opted to take on an older Pug, you will need to give him special consideration as he settles into his new home. A Pug may come from a house where the owner has died or is no longer able to care for his every need. However, the Pug is generally very amenable, and will soon learn to fit a new household. Try to establish a routine, which will help the dog to settle. For example, if you can stick to the same diet he is used to – and the same mealtimes – it will minimise the disruption. If there is any possibility of taking over any of

side and not getting his lead tangled round your legs. Start in a quiet place so your puppy can get used to the sound of passing traffic and then graduate to busier environments. Gradually, as your Pug gets older, the walk can be extended so he can get rid of some of his surplus energy.

CAR TRAVEL

Travelling with a Pug is usually no problem. Occasionally some may be travel sick, but if your puppy is accustomed to being in the car from an early age, he will enjoy outings in the car. It is best to travel with your Pug in a crate or a travelling box, making sure there is plenty of air

this old possessions, such as his bed, feeding bowls or toys, this will certainly help.

It will probably be advisable to have the Pug checked over by a vet to assess anything he may require in the way of medication. Eyes, ears and heart should be examined in case any treatment may be needed.

Introducing an older dog to your family, and to other pets, can be problematic if the dog is nervous, so it is important to take your time with this. Difficulties can also arise with house training. Generally, a Pug has a special place in the garden or yard where he relieves himself, and he will always go to the same spot. Until he is used to the new environment, he may feel disorientated, so you will need to take him out into the garden and praise him for performing, in the same way you would with a puppy.

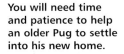

You will need time and patience to help an older Pug to settle into his new home.

THE BEST OF CARE

Chapter 5

The Pug is a relatively easy dog to care for; he has a short, low-maintenance coat, he thrives on moderate exercise, and he is rarely a fussy feeder. However, it is important to be aware that from the moment a Pug arrives in your home, you are responsible for all his needs.

UNDERSTANDING NUTRITION

Methods of feeding dogs go in and out of fashion, and most Pug owners and breeders will have their preferred diets. But when you are choosing a diet, you need to bear in mind the elements of nutrition that are essential for all dogs, regardless of breed, age or size.

PROTEINS

Proteins are composed of amino acids; these are the basic building blocks of life. During growth periods, such as pregnancy and lactation and puppyhood, a dog will need a diet with more protein, which will decrease as he reaches maturity. In most cases, a Pug in old age will do better on a diet with less protein. Too much protein in the diet can lead to its conversion by the body into fat, or in a growing animal in too swift a growth of muscle structure, which may lead to problems later in life. The main source of protein in a dog's diet is meat.

CARBOHYDRATES

Carbohydrates provide the body with energy, which may be converted into body fat. Carbohydrates are found in cereals such as wheat, rice, and corn, and in vegetables such as potatoes.

FATS

Fats are needed in the diet as they are a major source of energy. Dietary fats are composed of combinations of fatty acids, which are involved in many aspects of health.

WATER

A dog cannot survive for longer than a few days, or even hours, without water. A dog's daily water requirement will depend on many factors, including temperature, activity and type of food given as part of the diet. It is important, therefore, that adequate, fresh water is provided in the diet.

MINERALS AND VITAMINS

A number of minerals play a part in regulating body processes. Only very small amounts are needed; excess can result in ill health, as these can be toxic in high doses. Vitamins also help to regulate the body processes. Most cannot be made in the body and

A Pug needs a well-balanced diet to suit his age and lifestyle.

therefore must be provided in the diet.

CHOOSING A DIET
The lifestyle of the breeder or owner may have a bearing on the diet you choose.

COMPLETE FOOD
This is the ultimate convenience food: it is easy to feed, it has a long shelf life, and it is scientifically formulated so that it caters for all your dog's nutritional needs. If you feed a complete diet, you do not need to provide any supplements.

There is a great deal of choice when it comes to complete foods, which can be fed to puppies right through to adults and veterans. You can get complete food that is specially designed for Toy dogs, and you can also get prescription diets for dogs with specific health disorders. Complete food comes in the form of very small pellets or 'kibble' for puppies, graduating to a larger size for adults.

If you are a first-time owner, or you have a busy lifestyle, you will probably find that feeding a complete is the simplest option. If possible, ask your Pug's breeder to recommend a brand. A breeder has the advantage of caring for many different dogs of different ages, and will know what is most likely to suit your Pug.

CANNED
In the days before complete food, most dog owners fed a diet of canned meat and biscuit. Most dogs find this diet very palatable, but you need to make sure your Pug is getting the nutrition he needs. Canned food contains a high volume of moisture, and the ingredients also vary widely – there are some that have a high cereal content and relatively little meat. If you opt for this diet, read the list of ingredients that are printed on the can and seek further advice if you have any concerns.

HOME-MADE
Some owners prefer to design a home-made diet, which includes meat and vegetables, and carbohydrates in the form of biscuit, pasta or wholemeal bread. If you have the time, this can be very rewarding, but, again, you must ensure the diet is catering for all your Pug's needs.

The BARF (Biologically Appropriate Raw Food) diet is popular with some owners. This works on the premise that dogs in the wild ate the whole carcass of an animal – meat, bones, skin, etc. – and this should be

A complete diet is the ultimate convenience food for dogs.

Canned food is very appetising, but is has a high moisture content.

If you feed a homemade diet you must ensure you have the correct balance of nutrients.

replicated in their daily diet. This comes in the form of raw meat, bones, offal, plus fruit and vegetables. You can design your own BARF diet, or you can buy it from a BARF stockist.

FEEDING A PUG PUPPY

Some breeders prefer to start puppies on traditional foods, which include raw, scraped beef or a very fine mince. Puppies usually adore the beef and will suck it off a finger. Other meals for weaning puppies include cans of baby food, such as egg custard, baby rice pudding and baby porridge. These are easy to prepare in a microwave, and can be fed firstly from a spoon and then from a small dish. This way of feeding puppies is more time-consuming than giving a complete diet, but most puppies prefer a variety of foods rather than one type of food. Cooked

CHANGING DIETS

The breeder of your Pug puppy will have his or her own method of feeding and it is advisable not to change it when you take the new puppy home. A complete change of diet can upset the digestive system of the puppy and can cause problems with sickness and possibly diarrhoea.

If you do need to change the diet for any reason – you may have difficulty getting hold of a particular brand, or you may feel your puppy is not thriving – you must do so gradually. Add a little of the new food to the old diet, increasing the amount of new food over a period of seven days until you have made a complete transition. This method of switching diets should be employed, if the need arises, throughout your Pug's life.

Some breeders prefer to start puppies with a traditional diet of raw mince.

A CASE OF INDIGESTION

Sometimes a Pug puppy can be affected by a form of indigestion. The puppy will 'burp' and produce a lot of bile, which comes into the mouth and down the nose. When this happens, the nose is full of bile so the puppy may panic and run around with his mouth open. The bile needs to be wiped away from the nose and mouth, and the puppy should be allowed to settle quietly on your knee or in his playpen. A dose of milk of magnesia, which is an antacid, will help to neutralise the bile and will ease the problem.

This form of indigestion can occasionally happen in an adult Pug if he has gone too long without eating. Bile is produced and with no food to use it up it will have the same effect as on the puppy. This may never happen but it can be very frightening if the owner does not know what is happening,

chicken or cooked mince can be given with a little fine wholemeal biscuit food, which can be mixed in with meat and moistened with gravy.

The manufactured foods contain all necessary vitamins that are needed, but the alternative foods do not need extra additives and the puppies do just as well. Raw mince, eggs and the baby food have all the necessary nutrients.

In most cases, your Pug puppy will need three meals a day when he first arrives in your home. Remember, if you are feeding complete food, your puppy will need an abundant supply of fresh water. Puppies fed on fresh food and baby food will usually have milk to drink, but should also have a dish of water available.

Many breeders leave a dish of dry food in the puppy pen so that the puppies can help themselves whenever they want, while others prefer to give individual meals. Whether you adopt a free feeding regime or work around mealtimes is a matter of personal preference. However, it is very difficult to work out how much food your puppy is eating if it is being constantly topped up, so you may need to keep a check on your puppy's weight.

As your puppy gets older, you can cut out a meal – this usually happens at around four months. You can tell when your puppy is ready to reduce his meals as he will start leaving food or maybe show less interest in it at one of his mealtimes.

When your Pug is six months old, his meals can be reduced to two per day. If you find your Pug is a reluctant feeder, you can try feeding a complete food for one meal and raw mince or cooked mince can be given with a little wholemeal biscuit as another meal. A little variety in the diet can be beneficial, as Pugs do seem to tire of eating the same food.

ADULT FEEDING

Some people continue with two meals per day when the puppy becomes an adult, but others may cut down to one larger meal per day. This may well come down to convenience; Pugs seem to thrive on both regimes – although if your Pug loves his food, he may prefer two high spots during the course of the day!

BONES AND CHEWS

Bones are useful for occupying lively puppies – but they must be hard and uncooked. Rib and chicken bones should be avoided, as they can splinter and cause internal problems if sharp pieces are swallowed. Pugs of all ages enjoy chews, but they should be given only under supervision. A chew will soften with chewing, and, if chunks are swallowed, a Pug could easily choke. If a chew has become soft, it should be removed immediately.

You need to decide whether your Pug prefers a regime of one large meal or two smaller meals a day.

GROOMING

Grooming Pugs is not too difficult, but they do tend to cast a lot of hair at certain times. After a bitch has had puppies her coat will become rather thin and spiky, and after a bitch has been in season she tends to lose some coat. In some Pugs, the loss of coat will be very obvious, as the lack of undercoat shows up as missing patches. With other Pugs, hair shedding will not be obvious to anyone except the owner. The finer the coat, the less obvious it will be that a Pug is out of coat.

Black Pugs do not have an undercoat, so there is no obvious lack of hair. However, you may notice a black Pug going a rusty colour on the shoulders and hindquarters. If you come across a black Pug that has a fluffy undercoat, he will have some fawn ancestors, which accounts for the presence of undercoat.

ROUTINE CARE

BRUSHING AND COMBING

Your Pug should be groomed on a weekly basis with a stiff-bristle brush. This removes dirt and debris and is also good for the circulation. A pin brush or a fine-toothed comb is useful when your Pug is shedding his coat, as it helps to remove loose, dead hair. If your Pug is shedding his coat, it will help if you brush and comb more frequently. Bathing will also get rid of a lot of loose hair.

NOSE ROLL

The nose roll also needs to be kept clean. This is the area just above the nose where there is a deep fold of skin. The nose roll can vary a lot between Pugs – some have a small nose role, others may have a broken nose roll where the roll does not come all the way across the nose. As a result, some nose rolls need more care than others – some are frequently wet and dirty while others remain dry and clean! If the nose roll is allowed to remain wet or moist, the skin can become sore and an infection may develop. If this happens, you will need to seek help from the vet, who will prescribe ointment to clear up the problem.

The nose roll should be wiped clean on a regular basis. You can apply a little olive oil, which will help to keep the roll clean and also prevents it from becoming too dry. Avoid using Vaseline, as it tends to clog the roll and stops the air getting to it. Olive oil is also good for making the hair grow in the nose roll. The nose roll is covered with very fine hair, which sometimes disappears if the roll is not cleaned.

EYES

As part of your daily routine, wipe the eyes so they are clear of debris. Remember to use a separate wipe or piece of cotton-wool.(cotton) for each eye. The eyes should be bright and sparkling with no discharge. A small amount of tear-staining is nothing to worry about, but if you see evidence of a yellow discharge, your Pug will probably have an eye infection and will need treatment from a vet.

EARS

Ears need to be looked at regularly, too. Some Pugs have very clean ears while others need constant care. Ear-cleaning fluid can be obtained and can be used to clear wax out of the ear and to clean the ear lobe. Cotton buds can be useful, but should never be poked down the ear canal. Olive oil is also useful for cleaning out the ears.

NAILS

Nails can be difficult to deal with, as most Pugs seem to hate having them clipped or filed. Most will run a mile as soon as the nail-clippers appear! The best plan is to accustom your puppy to having his nails trimmed at an early stage. You can start by using scissors and then graduate to nail-clippers as the nail becomes tougher. Remember to reward your Pug if he co-operates, and, hopefully, he will learn to accept the procedure without too much fuss.

Clipping the nails should be done very carefully, as a vein runs through the middle of each nail; if this is cut too far back, it will bleed. The Breed Standard stipulates that a Pug should have black nails so the quick cannot be seen. However, it is quite easy to assess where the vein is, as the nail becomes thinner at the end, so can be trimmed a little further back from this. Some nails are much softer and will wear down naturally. But some Pugs have hard nails that do not wear down, even with plenty of road work for exercise. If this is the

ROUTINE CARE

A stiff, bristle brush will get rid of dirt and debris.

A pin brush is useful when the coat is shedding.

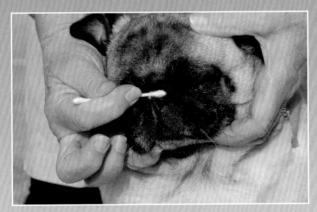

The nose roll must be cleaned on a daily basis.

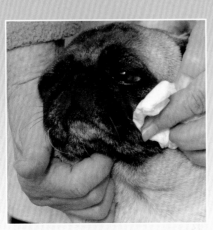

Wipe the eyes so they are free from debris.

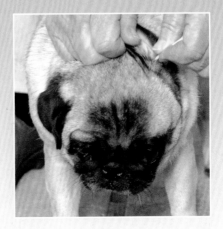

Clean the ears, but do not probe into the ear canal.

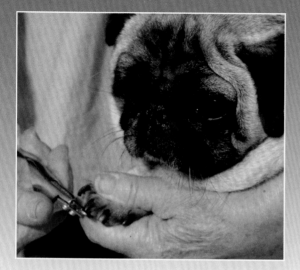

Nails will need trimming on a regular basis.

Accustom your Pug to teeth cleaning from an early age.

case, there is no option but to trim the nails, otherwise your Pug's feet will become very uncomfortable.

If the dewclaws have not been removed, they must also be trimmed, as if they get too long they can curl around and prod into the leg. Another problem with dewclaws can occur if a Pug has an eye irritation. The front leg comes up to rub the eye and the dewclaw can scratch the cornea, resulting in an ulcer. Treatment for an ulcer is often quite prolonged, needing drops and/or ointment prescribed by a vet. In bad cases the eye may even need to be stitched up. The plastic Elizabethan collar offers good protection from eye rubbing and can be useful following surgery.

TEETH

Teeth cleaning should also form part of your Pug's regular care. This is particularly necessary if your dog is fed a moist diet, which allows tartar to accumulate on the teeth. Again, this procedure is best started when your Pug is young so that he does not resent the attention. You can use a long-handled toothbrush, or, if you find it easier, you can buy a finger brush. You will also need some specially formulated toothpaste for dogs; this comes in different flavours, and most dogs seem to like the taste.

Start by rubbing a little toothpaste on the teeth, and praise your Pug if he does not struggle to get away. You can also give him a little treat to reward

him for co-operating. Progress to brushing the teeth, all the time praising your Pug and reassuring him. If you repeat this a number of times, your Pug will learn that he has nothing to fear from teeth cleaning.

Toy dogs do not always have the best teeth, so make sure you keep a close check to ensure the teeth are clean and the gums appear healthy. If you allow plaque and tartar to build up, you will have to ask your vet to clean the teeth under anaesthetic, which is costly and potentially risky for a Pug.

BATHING

Pugs do not need to be bathed too often, as the process tends to remove the natural oils from the coat. However, pale fawn Pugs do get dirty and will look several shades lighter after a bath. If your Pug is shedding his coat, you can hasten the process by bathing him and using a good-quality conditioner.

Some Pug puppies can be affected by dandruff. A lot of this can be combed out, but a bath using a specially formulated shampoo will get rid of it. Some people are affected by this dandruff and may develop itchy spots, but bathing your puppy will stop it happening. Sometimes this dandruff can harbour puppy mites. If your puppy is itching and he also has dandruff, ask your vet for advice, as mites can only be detected under a microscope.

STEP BY STEP
When you bath your Pug, make sure you have everything ready in advance to make the task as easy as possible. You will need:
- Shampoo
- Conditioner (optional)
- Towels
- A jug for diluting the conditioner
- As the Pug is small, you can bathe him in the sink, using a shower appliance, or you can use a shower cubicle.

Follow these instructions:
- Check that the water is warm and then soak the coat.
- Apply the shampoo and work into a rich lather.
- Rinse thoroughly.
- Dilute the conditioner according to the manufacturer's instructions and pour it over the coat.
- Work the conditioner into the coat and rinse again.
- Wrap your Pug in a towel so you absorb excess moisture before lifting him from the bath.
- If you have a hair-dryer, set it on a moderate heat and dry your Pug thoroughly.
- When you have finished, give him a thorough groom.

THE SHOW DOG
If you are going to a show, your Pug must look his very best. With a short-coated breed, this is relatively straightforward, but as the judges carries out a 'hands on' examination, you want to make sure your Pug is immaculate. You will need to bath your Pug a couple of days before the show, and you will need to clean his ears and nose roll, and also make sure his eyes are wiped clear of debris. The nails must be clipped to show off the correct shape of the feet.

A show dog must look immaculate when he is exhibited in the ring.

EXERCISING YOUR PUG

A Pug puppy needs very little exercise – in fact, he will get as much exercise as he needs from playing in the garden. However, you will need to train him to walk on a lead, as a puppy needs to be fully socialised, experiencing all the sights and sounds of the outside world.

For information on training and socialisation, see Chapter Six.

When your Pug becomes an adult, you can work out a regime of exercise that will suit you both. This is a very adaptable breed, and if you enjoy walking, your Pug will be happy to accompany you on long excursions. However, he will be equally content with shorter walks, as long as he has the stimulation of going to new places. There is also the fair-weather brigade, who will swiftly lose their enthusiasm for going out if it is raining!

Pugs do not usually like water and will often go out of their way to avoid puddles, although there are some that will be happy to splash around in water and may even enjoy swimming. If your Pug is a swimmer, take care that he is only allowed to go in safe stretches of water, where there are no strong currents. You should also check that there is an easy route out of the water before you let him take the plunge!

Another way of giving exercise is to throw a toy or ball to see if your Pug will retrieve. Some will bring the toy back and wait for it to be thrown again. If you are playing with a ball, it must be small enough to be picked up easily, or it should be a soft, plastic type of ball, which your Pug can get hold of with his teeth. Tennis balls are too big – a Pug cannot fit one in his mouth, which makes it impossible to retrieve.

A specially designed exit means that these Pugs have the freedom to go in and out whenever they choose.

PUGS AND EXERCISE

A fit Pug is surprisingly energetic and will enjoy free running exercise.

Most Pugs dislike getting wet – but there are some that enjoy having a splash around.

An older Pug will still enjoy his exercise, but make sure he does not overdo it.

A cosy bed will be greatly appreciated.

THE OLDER PUG

As your Pug gets older, his needs will change as he gradually starts to slow down. His need for exercise will decrease and he may prefer sniffing around in the garden rather than going out for a walk.

An older Pug will often sleep a lot of the time and will appreciate having a warm, cosy bed.

Hopefully, your Pug will still enjoy his food. If you are feeding one meal a day, he may prefer two smaller meals, which will be easier to digest. He may be perfectly happy to stay on his normal diet and will be upset by a change. However, special food can be obtained for the veterans; some have extra vitamins and other supplements that help with

conditions such as arthritis, which may affect the older dog.

Some Pugs seem to age more quickly than others. Some dogs may show the first signs of ageing from eight years of age, while others remain very active until 11 years or more. With luck, your Pug will live into his teens – and I know of many 14- and 15-year-old Pugs who enjoy a high-quality life.

LETTING GO

The decision to end your Pug's life is heartbreaking – but it is your duty as a caring owner to try to be as objective as possible. It is the day-to-day quality of life that must be considered. Some think that if a Pug is still enjoying his food, that is sufficient reason to keep going. But the Pug is an active dog that likes to be involved in his owner's life. If he cannot move around freely and be included in family activities, he will be miserable. You also need to consider if your Pug is in pain; it is unfair to keep a dog alive when he is suffering just because you cannot bear to lose him.

The best plan is to talk to your vet, who will give a clear, objective opinion and will help you to make the right decision, at the right time.

In time, you will be able to look back and remember all the happy times you spent with your beloved Pug.

TRAINING & SOCIALISATION

Chapter 6

When you decided to bring a Pug into your life, you probably had dreams of how it was going to be, enjoying the loving companionship of this exceptional little Toy dog who would *always* be well behaved, *always* delighted to see you, and *always* perfectly adapted to your lifestyle.

There is no doubt that you can achieve this – well, most of this – with a Pug, but like anything that is worth having, you must be prepared to put in the work. A Pug, regardless of whether he is a puppy or an adult, does not come ready trained, understanding exactly what you want from him. A Pug has to learn his place in your family and he must discover what is acceptable behaviour.

We have a great starting point in that the breed has an outstanding temperament. The Pug's role in life is to be a companion and, as such, his greatest desire is to be with people and to please them. He is intelligent and quick to learn, but watch out for that mischievous streak. Most owners would agree that if you give your Pug an inch, he will certainly take a mile!

THE FAMILY PACK

Dogs have been domesticated for some 14,000 years, but, luckily for us, they have inherited and retained behaviour from their distant ancestor – the wolf. For many Pug owners, this is a difficult concept to grasp, because the Pug is such a people dog, who thrives on the comforts of home life. But although you cannot envisage your Pug living in the wild, he still owes much to his ancestry and is born with the survival skills and the mentality of a meat-eating predator who hunts in a pack. A wolf living in a pack owes its existence to mutual co-operation and an acceptance of a hierarchy, as this ensures both food and protection. A domesticated dog living in a family pack has exactly the same outlook. He wants food, companionship, and leadership – and it is your job to provide for these needs.

YOUR ROLE

Theories about dog behaviour and methods of training go in and out of fashion, but in reality, nothing has changed from the day when wolves ventured in from the wild to join the family circle. The wolf (and equally the dog) accepts a subservient place in the family pack in return for food and protection. In a dog's eyes, you are his leader and he relies on you to make all the important decisions. This does

Do you have what it takes to be a firm, fair and consistent leader?

accept his place in the family pack, he must respect his leader as the decision-maker. A low-ranking pack animal does not question authority; he is perfectly happy to see someone else shoulder the responsibility. Problems will only arise if you cut a poor figure as leader and the dog feels he should mount a challenge for the top-ranking role.

HOW TO BE A GOOD LEADER

There are a number of guidelines to follow to establish yourself in the role of leader in a way that your Pug understands and respects. If you have a puppy, you may think you don't have to take this on board for a few months, but that would be a big mistake. With a Pug it is absolutely essential to start as you mean to go on. The behaviour he learns as a puppy will continue throughout his adult life, which means that undesirable behaviour can be very difficult to rectify.

When your Pug first arrives in his new home, follow these guidelines:

- **Keep it simple:** Decide on the rules you want your Pug to obey and always make it 100 per cent clear what is acceptable, and what is unacceptable, behaviour.

- **Be consistent:** If you are not consistent about enforcing rules, how can you expect your Pug to take you seriously? There is nothing worse than allowing your Pug to jump on the sofa one moment and then scolding him the next time he does it

not mean that you have to act like a dictator or a bully. You are accepted as a leader, without argument, as long as you have the right credentials.

The first part of the job is easy. You are the provider and you are therefore respected because you

supply food. In a Pug's eyes, you must be the ultimate hunter, because a day never goes by when you cannot find food. The second part of the leader's job description is straightforward, but for some reason we find it hard to achieve. In order for a dog to

because he is muddy. As far as the Pug is concerned, he may as well try it on because he cannot predict your reaction. Bear in mind, inconsistency leads to insecurity.

- **Get your timing right:** If you are rewarding your Pug and equally if you are reprimanding him, you must respond within one to two seconds otherwise the dog will not link his behaviour with your reaction (see page 84).

- **Read your dog's body language:** Find out how to read body language and facial expressions (see page 82) so that you understand your Pug's feelings and intentions. This can take some skill with a Pug, who has a short, broad muzzle, a pushed-in nose, and wrinkles. But when you get in tune with the breed, you will be able to detect his moods and feelings.

- **Be aware of your own body language:** When you ask your Pug to do something, do not be confrontational, giving him direct eye contact. He will see this as threatening behaviour and will not be willing to co-operate. You can also help your dog to learn by using your body language to communicate with him. For example, if you want your dog to come to you, open your arms out and look inviting. If you want your dog to stay, use a hand signal (palm flat, facing the dog) so you are effectively 'blocking' his advance.

- **Tone of voice:** Dogs do not speak English; they learn by associating a word with the required action. However, they are very receptive to tone of voice, so you can use your voice to praise him or to correct undesirable behaviour. If you are pleased with your Pug, praise him to the skies in a warm, happy voice. If you want to stop him raiding the bin, use a deep, stern voice when you say "No".

- **Give one command only:** If you keep repeating a command, or keeping changing it, your Pug will think you are babbling and will probably ignore you. If your Pug does not respond the first time you ask, make it simple by using a treat to lure him into position and then you can reward him for a correct response.

- **Daily reminders:** A mischievous Pug may forget his manners from time to time and an adolescent dog may attempt to challenge your authority (see page 105). Rather than coming down on your Pug like a ton of bricks when he does something wrong, try to prevent bad manners by daily reminders of good manners. For example:

i. Do not let your dog barge ahead of you when you are going through a door.

ii. Do not let him leap out of

Keep it clear and simple so your Pug understands what is acceptable behaviour.

If you watch two Pugs interacting, you will start to understand their body language.

the car the moment you open the door (which could be potentially lethal, as well as being disrespectful).

iii. Do not let him eat from your hand when you are at the table.

iv. Do not let him 'win' a toy at the end of a play session and then make off with it. You 'own' his toys and you 'allow' him to play with them. Your Pug must learn to give up a toy when you ask.

UNDERSTANDING YOUR PUG

Body language is an important means of communication between dogs, which they use to make friends, to assert status and to avoid conflict. It is important to get on your dog's wavelength by understanding his body language and reading his facial expressions. This will also help you to interpret other dogs' behaviour so you can tell if their intentions are friendly or otherwise when they are interacting with your Pug.

• A positive, upright body posture indicates a happy, confident dog. The Pug has a twist in his tail, which means he cannot wag it as such, but he will wriggle his rear end, which will make his tail move.

• A crouched body posture with ears back and tail down between the legs show that a dog is being submissive. A dog may do this when he is being told off or if a more assertive dog approaches him.

• A bold dog will stand tall, looking strong and alert, with ears well forward.

• A dog who raises his hackles (lifting the fur along his topline) is trying to look as scary as possible.

• A playful dog will go down on his front legs while standing on his hind legs in a bow position. This friendly invitation says: "I'm no threat, let's play."

• A dominant, aggressive dog will meet other dogs with a hard stare. If he is challenged, he may bare his teeth and growl and the corners of his mouth will be drawn forward. His ears will be forward and he will appear tense in every muscle.

• A nervous dog will often show

aggressive behaviour as a means of self-protection. If threatened, this dog will lower his head and flatten his ears. The corners of his mouth may be drawn back and he may bark or whine.

- The Pug has his own unique way of expressing himself. Known as the 'Pug run', you will suddenly see your Pug take off with his tail straight between his legs, and his back legs tucked under his bottom. He will circle madly for a few minutes, and then come to an abrupt halt.

GIVING REWARDS

Why should your Pug do as you ask? If you follow the guidelines given above, your Pug should respect your authority, but what about the time when he is playing with a new doggy friend or has found a really enticing scent? The answer is that you must always be the most interesting, the most attractive and the most irresistible person in your Pug's eyes. It would be nice to think that you could achieve this by personality alone, but most of us need a little extra help. You need to find out what is the biggest reward for your dog. In most cases, a Pug will be motivated to work for a food reward, although some prefer a game with a favourite toy. But whatever reward you use, make sure it is something that your dog really wants.

When you are teaching a new exercise, you should reward your Pug frequently. When he knows the exercise or command, reward him randomly to keep him on his toes. This will mean that he does not become bored and 'switch off' but keeps on responding to you in a positive manner.

If your Pug does something extra special, like coming back the moment you call, make sure he really knows how pleased you are by giving him a handful of treats or having an extra-long play with his favourite toy. If he gets a bonanza reward, he is more likely to come back on future occasions because you have proved to be even more rewarding than his previous activity.

TOP TREATS

Some trainers grade treats depending on what they are asking the dog to do. A dog may get a low-grade treat (such as a piece of dry food) to reward good behaviour on a random basis, such as sitting when you open a door or allowing you to examine his teeth. High-grade treats (which may be cooked liver, sausage or cheese) may be reserved for training new exercises, or for use in the park when you want a really good recall, for example.

Whatever type of treat you use, you should remember to subtract it from your Pug's daily food ration. Pugs are prone to obesity. Fat dogs are lethargic, more likely to suffer from health problems and will almost certainly have a shorter life expectancy, so reward your Pug, but always keep a check on his figure!

For some Pugs, a game with a favourite toy is a top reward.

HOW DO DOGS LEARN?

It is not difficult to get inside your Pug's head and understand how he learns, as it is not dissimilar to the way we learn. Dogs learn by conditioning: they find out that specific behaviours produce specific consequences. This is known as operant conditioning or consequence learning. Consequences have to be immediate or clearly linked to the behaviour, as a dog sees the world in terms of action and result. Dogs will quickly learn if an action has a bad consequence or a good consequence.

Dogs also learn by association. This is known as classical conditioning or association learning. It is the type of learning made famous by Pavlov's experiment with dogs. Pavlov presented dogs with food and measured their salivary response (how much they drooled). Then he rang a bell just before presenting the food. At first, the dogs did not salivate until the food was presented. But after a while they learnt that the sound of the bell meant that food was coming and so they salivated when they heard the bell. A dog needs to learn the association in order for it to have any meaning. For example, a dog that has never seen a lead before will be completely indifferent to it. A dog that has learnt that a lead means he is going for a walk will get excited the second he sees the lead; he has learnt to associate a lead with a walk.

BE POSITIVE

The most effective method of training dogs is to use their ability to learn by consequence and to teach that the behaviour you want produces a good consequence. For example, if you ask your Pug to "Sit" and reward him with a treat, he will learn that it is worth his while to sit on command because it will lead to a treat. He is far more likely to repeat the behaviour, and the behaviour will become stronger, because it results in a positive

THE CLICKER REVOLUTION

Karen Pryor pioneered the technique of clicker training when she was working with dolphins. It is very much a continuation of Pavlov's work and makes full use of association learning. Karen wanted to mark 'correct' behaviour at the precise moment it happened. She found it was impossible to toss a fish to a dolphin when it was in mid-air, when she wanted to reward it. Her aim was to establish a conditioned response so the dolphin knew that it had performed correctly and a reward would follow.

The solution was the clicker: a small matchbox-shaped training aid, with a metal tongue that makes a click when it is pressed. To begin with, the dolphin had to learn that a click meant that food was coming. The dolphin then learnt that it must 'earn' a click in order to get a reward. Clicker training has been used with many different animals, most particularly with dogs, and it has proved hugely successful. It is a great aid for pet owners and is also widely used by professional trainers who teach highly specialised skills.

outcome. This method of training is known as positive reinforcement and it generally leads to a happy, co-operative dog that is willing to work and a handler who has fun training their dog.

The opposite approach is negative reinforcement. This is far less effective and often results in a poor relationship between dog and owner. In this method of training, you ask your Pug to "Sit" and if he does not respond, you deliver a sharp yank on the training collar or push his rear to the ground. The dog learns that not responding to your command has a bad consequence and he may be less likely to ignore you in the future. However, it may well have a bad consequence for you, too. A dog that is treated in this way may associate harsh handling with the handler and become aggressive or fearful. Instead of establishing a pattern of willing co-operation, you are establishing a relationship built on coercion.

GETTING STARTED

When you train your Pug, you will develop your own techniques as you get to know what motivates him. You may decide to get involved with clicker training or you may prefer to go for a simple command-and-reward formula. It does not matter what form of training you use, as long as it is based on positive, reward-based methods.

There are a few important guidelines to bear in mind when you are training your Pug:

- Find a training area that is free from distractions, particularly when you are just starting out. A Pug may become distracted by sights and smells in the garden, so it may be easier to train him indoors to begin with.
- Keep training sessions short, especially with young puppies that have very short attention spans.
- Do not train if you are in a bad mood or if you are on a tight schedule – the training session will be doomed to failure.
- If you are using a toy as a reward, make sure it is only available when you are training. In this way it has an added value for your Pug.
- If you are using food treats, make sure they are bite-size and easy to swallow; you don't

want to hang about while your Pug chews on his treat.
- Do not attempt to train your Pug after he has eaten, or soon after returning from exercise. He will either be too full up to care about food treats or too tired to concentrate.
- When you are training, move around your allocated area so that your dog does not think that an exercise can only be performed in one place.
- If your Pug is finding an exercise difficult, try not to get frustrated. Go back a step and praise him for his effort. You will probably find he is more successful when you try again at the next training session.
- If a training session is not going well – either because you are in the wrong frame of mind or the

Do not attempt to train your Pug after he has just eaten, or after exercise, as he will not want to know.

dog is not focusing – ask your Pug to do something you know he can do (such as a trick he enjoys performing) and then you can reward him with a food treat or a play with his favourite toy, ending the session on a happy, positive note.

- The Pug has a stubborn streak, which can make training more difficult. However, the worst mistake you can make is to become confrontational, eye-balling your Pug and demanding his co-operation. This is a dog with strong will, and he will be able to keep up his policy of non-co-operation for longer than you think. The secret is to keep everything light-hearted and fun. If training is treated as a big game, you will soon find you have a willing pupil.

- Do not train for too long. You need to end a training session on a high, with your Pug wanting more, rather than making him sour by asking too much from him.

In the exercises that follow, clicker training is introduced and followed, but all the exercises will work without the use of a clicker.

INTRODUCING A CLICKER

This is easy, and the intelligent Pug will learn about the clicker in record time! It can be combined with attention training, which is a very useful tool and can be used on many different occasions.

- Prepare some treats and go to an area that is free from distractions. Allow your Pug to wander, and, when he stops to look at you, click and reward by throwing him a treat. This means he will not crowd you, but will go looking for the treat. Repeat a couple of times. If your Pug is very easily distracted, you may need to start this exercise with the dog on a lead.

- After a few clicks, your Pug will understand that if he hears a click, he will get a treat. He must now learn that he must 'earn' a click. This time, when

The clever Pug will be quick to learn that when he hears a "click" a reward will follow.

With a little practice, your can teach your Pug to sit on command.

your Pug looks at you, wait a little longer before clicking and then reward him. If your Pug is on a lead but responding well, try him off the lead.

- When your Pug is working for a click and giving you his attention, you can introduce a cue or command word, such as "Watch". Repeat a few times, using the cue. You now have a Pug that understands the clicker and will give you his attention when you ask him to "Watch".

TRAINING EXERCISES
Compared to some of the working breeds, the Pug is not a naturally biddable dog. He was not bred to work *for* people, but to be *with* people. He wants to please because he adores his human family and wants to bask in their admiration. But he will not see the point in being drilled, army style, to produce 'perfect' behaviour.

When training a Pug, use high-value treats and make sure exercises do not become dull and repetitive. Work at your tone of voice so everything sounds like fun – and always quit while you are ahead!

THE SIT
This is one of the easiest exercise to teach, so it is rewarding for both you and your Pug.

- Choose a tasty treat and hold it just above your puppy's nose. As he looks up at the treat, he will naturally go into the 'Sit'. As soon as he is in position, reward him.
- Repeat the exercise, and, when your pup understands what you want, introduce the "Sit" command.
- You can practise the Sit exercise at mealtimes by holding out the bowl and waiting for your dog to sit. Most Pugs learn this one very quickly!

THE DOWN

Work hard at this exercise because a reliable 'Down' is useful in many different situations, and an instant 'Down' can be a lifesaver.

- You can start with your dog in a 'Sit', or it is just as effective to teach it when the dog is standing. Hold a treat just below your puppy's nose and slowly lower it towards the ground. The treat acts as a lure and your puppy will follow it, first going down on his forequarters and then bringing his hindquarters down as he tries to get the treat.

- Make sure you close your fist around the treat and only reward your puppy with the treat when he is in the correct position. If your puppy is reluctant to go 'Down', you can apply gentle pressure on his shoulders to encourage him to go into the correct position.
- When your puppy is following the treat and going into position, introduce a verbal command.
- Build up this exercise over a period of time, each time waiting a little longer before giving the reward, so the puppy learns to stay in the 'Down' position.

THE RECALL

It is never too soon to begin training your Pug the recall. Many Pug owners make the mistake of thinking that because they have a little dog, he will trot alongside them on walks and will not stray too far away. However, your Pug is a dog, and he has all the canine instincts, such as following scents and wanting to go up and meet other dogs. There is nothing wrong with this – but when your Pug has had his 'dog time', you want a ready response to the recall command.

Hopefully, the breeder will have already started recall training by calling the puppies in from

The down is an extension of the sit exercise, and you can use a treat to lure your Pug into position.

outside and rewarding them with some treats scattered on the floor. But even if this has not been the case, you will find that a puppy arriving in his new home is highly responsive. His chief desire is to follow you and be with you. Capitalise on this from day one by getting your pup's attention and calling him to you in a bright, excited tone of voice.

- Practise in the garden. When your puppy is busy exploring, get his attention by calling his name and, as he runs towards you, introduce the verbal command "Come". Make sure you sound happy and exciting so your puppy wants to come to you. When he responds, give him lots of praise.

- If your puppy is slow to respond, try running away a few paces, or jumping up and down. It doesn't matter how silly you look, the key issue is to get your puppy's attention and then to make yourself irresistible!

- In a dog's mind, coming when called should be regarded as the best fun because he knows he is always going to be rewarded. Never make the mistake of telling your dog off, no matter how slow he is to respond, as you will undo all your previous hard work.

- When you call your Pug to you, make sure he comes up close enough to be touched. He must understand that "Come" means that he should come right up to you, otherwise he will think that he can approach and then veer off

The aim is to build up an enthusiastic response to the recall.

when it suits him.

- When you are free running your dog, make sure you have his favourite toy or a pocket full of treats so you can reward him at intervals throughout the walk when you call him to you. Do not allow your dog to free

run and only call him back at the end of the walk to clip on his lead. An intelligent Pug will soon realise that the recall means the end of his walk and then end of fun – so who can blame him for not wanting to come back?

SECRET WEAPON

You can build up a strong recall by using another form of association learning. Buy a whistle and when you are giving your Pug his food, peep on the whistle. You can choose the type of signal you want to give: two short peeps or one long whistle, for example. Within a matter of days, your dog will learn that the sound of the whistle means that food is coming.

Now transfer the lesson outside. Arm yourself with some tasty treats and the whistle. Allow your Pug to run free in the garden, and, after a couple of minutes, use the whistle. The dog has already learnt to associate the whistle with food, so he will come towards you. Immediately reward him with a treat and lots of praise. Repeat the lesson a few times in the garden, so you are confident that your dog is responding before trying it in the park. Make sure you always have some treats in your pocket when you go for a walk and your dog will quickly learn how rewarding it is to come to you.

TRAINING LINE

This is the equivalent of a very long lead, which you can buy at a pet store, or you can make your own with a length of rope. The training line is attached to your Pug's collar and should be around 15 feet (4.5 metres) in length.

The purpose of the training line is to prevent your Pug from disobeying you so that he never has the chance to get into bad habits. For example, when you call your Pug and he ignores you, you can immediately pick up the end of the training line and call him again. By picking up the line you will have attracted his attention and if you call in an excited, happy voice, your Pug will come to you. The moment he reaches you, give him a tasty treat so he is instantly rewarded for making the 'right' decision.

When you have reinforced the correct behaviour a number of times, your dog will build up a strong recall and you will not need to use a training line.

WALKING ON A LOOSE LEAD

This is a simple exercise, which should not be problematical with a Pug. Although the Pug is a small dog, he is strongly built, but it is very rare of a Pug to use his strength against you. A more common problem is a dog who wants to stop and sniff every interesting smell, and so walking on lead is a frustrating stop-start experience. For this reason, you should teach your Pug to walk on a loose lead, using treats and rewarding correct behaviour. Do not allow your Pug to get into bad habits; he should be happy to walk alongside you so that lead walking is a pleasant experience for both of you.

- In the early stages of lead training, allow your puppy to pick his route and follow him. He will get used to the feeling of being 'attached' to you and has no reason to put up any resistance.
- Next, find a toy or a tasty treat and show it to your puppy. Let him follow the treat/toy for a few paces and then reward him.
- Build up the amount of time your pup will walk with you, and, when he is walking nicely by your side, introduce the verbal command "Heel" or "Close". Give lots of praise when your pup is in the correct position.

- When your pup is walking alongside you, keep focusing his attention on you by using his name and then rewarding him when he looks at you. If it is going well, introduce some changes of direction.
- Do not attempt to take your puppy out on the lead until you have mastered the basics at home. You need to be confident that your puppy accepts the lead and will focus his attention on you, when requested, before you face the challenge of a busy environment.
- If you are heading somewhere special, such as the park, your Pug may try to surge ahead

because he is impatient to get there. If this happens, stop, call your dog to you and do not set off again until he is in the correct position. It may take time, but your Pug will eventually realise that it is more productive to walk by your side than to run ahead.

STAYS

This may not be the most exciting exercise, but it is one of the most useful. There are many occasions when you want your Pug to stay in position, even if it is only for a few seconds. The classic example is when you want your Pug to stay in the back of the car until you have clipped on

If your Pugs learn to be well behaved on the lead, outings will be a pleasure even when you are going out mob-handed!

his lead. Some trainers use the verbal command "Stay" when the dog is to stay in position for an extended period of time, and

Keep your Pug on lead when you start teaching the Stay exercise.

"Wait" if the dog is to stay in position for a few seconds until you give the next command. Other trainers use a universal "Stay" to cover all situations. It all comes down to personal preference, and as long as you are consistent, your dog will understand the command he is given.

- Put your puppy in a 'Sit' or a 'Down' and use a hand signal (flat palm, facing the dog) to show he is to stay in position. Step a pace away from the dog. Wait a second, step back and reward him. If you have a lively pup, you may find it easier to train this exercise on the lead.
- Repeat the exercise, gradually increasing the distance you can leave your dog. When you return to your dog's side, praise him quietly and release him with a command, such as "OK".
  - Remember to keep your body language very still when you are training this exercise and avoid eye contact with your dog. Work on this exercise over a period of time and you will build up a really reliable 'Stay'.

SOCIALISATION

While your Pug is mastering basic obedience exercises, there is other, equally important work to do with him. A Pug is not only becoming a part of your home and family, he is becoming a member of the community. He needs to be able to live in the outside world, coping calmly with every new situation that comes his way. It is your job to introduce him to as many different experiences as possible and to encourage him to behave in an appropriate manner. The Pug is an even-tempered dog and does not go looking for trouble, but the more he experiences while he is growing up, the more tolerant he will be of people, dogs and livestock, as well as all the sights and sounds of modern life.

In order to socialise your Pug effectively, it is helpful to understand how his brain is developing and then you will get a perspective on how he sees the world.

CANINE SOCIALISATION
(Birth to 7 weeks)
This is the time when a dog learns how to be a dog. By interacting with his mother and his littermates, a young pup learns about leadership and submission. He learns to read body posture so that he understands the intentions of his mother and his siblings. A puppy that is taken away from his litter too early may always have behavioural problems with other dogs, either being fearful or aggressive.

In the first socialisation period, puppies learn to interact with each other, and with their mother.

SOCIALISATION PERIOD
(7 to 12 weeks)

This is the time to get cracking and introduce your Pug puppy to as many different experiences as possible. This includes meeting different people, other dogs and animals, seeing new sights and hearing a range of sounds, from the vacuum cleaner to the roar of traffic. A puppy learns very quickly and what he learns will stay with him for the rest of his life. This is the best time for a puppy to move to a new home, as he is adaptable and ready to form deep bonds.

FEAR-IMPRINT PERIOD
(8 to 11 weeks)

This occurs during the socialisation period and it can be the cause of problems if it is not handled carefully. If a pup is exposed to a frightening or painful experience, it will lead to lasting impressions. Obviously, you will attempt to avoid frightening situations, such as your pup being bullied by a mean-spirited older dog, or a firework going off, but you cannot always protect your puppy from the unexpected. If your pup has a nasty experience, the best plan is to make light of it and distract him by offering him a treat or a game. The pup will take the lead from you and will be reassured that there is nothing to worry about. If you mollycoddle him and sympathise with him, he is far more likely to retain the memory of his fear.

SENIORITY PERIOD
(12 to 16 weeks)

During this period, your puppy starts to cut the apron strings and becomes more independent. He will test out his status to find out who is the pack leader: him or you. Bad habits, such as play biting, which may have been seen as endearing a few weeks earlier, should be firmly discouraged. Remember to use positive, reward-based training, but make sure your puppy knows that you are the leader and must be respected.

SECOND FEAR-IMPRINT PERIOD (6 to 14 months)

This period is not as critical as the first fear-imprint period, but it should still be handled carefully.

As a puppy grows up, he will start to question the status quo.

During this time your Pug may appear apprehensive, or he may show fear of something familiar. You may feel as if you have taken a backwards step, but if you adopt a calm, positive manner, your Pug will see that there is nothing to be frightened of. Do not make your dog confront the thing that frightens him. Simply distract his attention, and give him something else to think about, such as obeying a simple command, such as "Sit" or "Down". This will give you the opportunity to praise and reward your dog and will help to boost his confidence.

YOUNG ADULTHOOD AND MATURITY (1 to 4 years)

The timing of this phase depends on the size of the dog: the bigger the dog, the later it is. This period coincides with a dog's increased size and strength, mental as well as physical. Some dogs, particularly those with a dominant nature, will test your leadership again and may become aggressive towards other dogs. Firmness and continued training are essential at this time, so that your Pug accepts his status in the family pack.

IDEAS FOR SOCIALISATION

When you are socialising your Pug, you want him to experience as many different situations as possible. Try out some of the following ideas, which will ensure your Pug has an all-round education.

If you are taking on a rescued dog and have little knowledge of his background, it is important to work through a programme of socialisation. A young puppy soaks up new experiences like a sponge, but an older dog can still learn. If a rescued dog shows fear or apprehension, treat him in exactly the same way as you would treat a youngster who is going through the second fear-imprint period.

- Accustom your puppy to household noises, such as the vacuum cleaner, the television and the washing machine.
- Ask visitors to come to the door, wearing different types of clothing – for example, wearing a hat, a long raincoat, or carrying a stick or an umbrella.
- If you do not have children at home, make sure your Pug has a chance to meet and play with them. Most Pugs have a natural affinity with children, but little humans that run about and shout in high-pitched voices can seem rather strange to begin with. Go to a local park and watch children in the play area. You will not be able to take your Pug inside the play area, but he will see children playing and will get used to their shouts of excitement.
- Attend puppy classes. These are designed for puppies between the ages of 12 to 20 weeks and give puppies a chance to play and interact together in a controlled, supervised environment. Your vet will have details of a local class.

TRAINING CLUBS

It is a good idea to take your Pug to training classes so he learns to focus on you despite other distractions. The main distraction will be working alongside other dogs. The Pug is friendly and out-going in most situations, but, when on-lead, he sometimes feels the need to bark at other dogs. A well-socialised Pug who is used to meeting lots of different dogs in a controlled environment will learn good canine manners, meeting and greeting other dogs quietly and calmly on-lead and off-lead.

There are lots of training clubs to choose from. Your vet will probably have details of clubs in your area or you can ask dog-owning friends if they attend a club. Alternatively, use the internet to find out more information. But how do you know if the club is any good?

Before you take your dog, ask if you can go to a class as an observer and find out the following:

- What experience does the instructor(s) have?
- Do they have experience with Pugs?
- Is the class well organised and are the dogs reasonably quiet? (A noisy class indicates an unruly atmosphere, which will not be conducive to learning.)
- Are there a number of classes to suit dogs of different ages and abilities?
- Are positive, reward-based training methods used?
- Does the club train for the Good Citizen Scheme (see page 104)?

If you are not happy with the training club, find another one. An inexperienced instructor who cannot handle a number of dogs in a confined environment can do more harm than good.

A well socialised Pug will react calmly and confidently in all situations.

The adaptable Pug will be happy to fit in with whatever you want to do – including travelling on the roof of a barge...

- Take a walk around some quiet streets, such as a residential area, so your Pug can get used to the sound of traffic. As he becomes more confident, progress to busier areas. Remember, your lead is like a live wire and your feelings will travel directly to your Pug. Assume a calm, confident manner and your puppy will take the lead from you and have no reason to be fearful.
- Go to a railway station. You don't have to get on a train if you don't need to, but your Pug will have the chance to experience trains, people wheeling luggage, loudspeaker announcements and going up and down stairs and over railway bridges.
- If you live in the town, plan a trip to the country. You can enjoy a day out and provide an opportunity for your Pug to see livestock, such as sheep, cattle and horses.
- One of the best places for socialising a dog is at a country fair. There will be crowds of people, livestock in pens, tractors, bouncy castles, fairground rides and food stalls.
- When your dog is over 20 weeks of age, locate a training class for adult dogs. You may find that your local training club has both puppy and adult classes.

THE ADOLESCENT PUG
It happens to every dog – and every owner. One minute you have a well-behaved, easy-going youngster, and the next you have an adolescent who has developed a 'selective' memory, only responding to commands when he feels like it.

A Pug male will show

It is not unusual for an adolescent Pug to challenge your authority.

adolescent behaviour at around seven months of age and will not be fully mature until he is 18 months or even two years old. During this interim period, a Pug may become more assertive as he pushes the boundaries to see if he can achieve top dog status.

If you have another male dog, the adolescent may try to dominate him; if you have a female, he may try to 'ride' her. Scent marking – when a male cocks his leg to leave a few drops of urine as his own personal calling card – will usually start at around 10 months.

Female Pugs have their first season at any time between six months and 12 months of age. In the run-up to coming into season, and while she is in season, a female may become a little withdrawn and preoccupied. During her adolescence, she may try to elevate her status – particularly if you have other female dogs at home – and she may well take to pleasing herself rather than co-operating with you. A female Pug generally reaches full maturity at around 18 months to two years of age.

This can be a trying time, but it is important to retain a sense of perspective.

Try to look at difficult situations from the dog's perspective and respond to uncharacteristic behaviour with firmness and consistency. Just like a teenager, an adolescent Pug feels the need to flex his muscles and challenge the status quo. But if you show that you are a strong leader (see page 80) and are quick to reward good behaviour, your Pug will be happy to accept you as his protector and provider.

A Pug can be demanding in his behaviour in order to get your attention.

WHEN THINGS GO WRONG

Positive, reward-based training has proved to be the most effective method of teaching dogs, but what happens when your Pug does something wrong and you need to show him that his behaviour is unacceptable? The old-fashioned school of dog training used to rely on the powers of punishment and negative reinforcement. A dog who raided the bin, for example, was smacked. Now we have learnt that it is not only unpleasant and cruel to hit a dog, it is also ineffective. If you hit a dog for stealing, he is more than likely to see you as the bad consequence of stealing, so he may raid the bin again, but probably not when you are around. If he raided the bin some time before you discovered it, he will be even more confused by your punishment, as he will not relate your response to his 'crime'.

A more commonplace example is when a dog fails to respond to a recall in the park. When the dog eventually comes back, the owner puts the dog on the lead and goes straight home to punish the dog for his poor response. Unfortunately, the dog will have a different interpretation. He does not think: "I won't ignore a recall command because the bad consequence is the end of my play in the park." He thinks:

"Coming to my owner resulted in the end of playtime – therefore coming to my owner has a bad consequence, so I won't do that again."

There are a number of strategies to tackle undesirable behaviour – and they have nothing to do with harsh handling.

Ignoring bad behaviour: The Pug is a natural attention-seeker, and this is part of the breed's charm. But your Pug must learn to ask for attention rather than demand it. For example, a Pug that barks when he wants to be lifted up on to the sofa for a cuddle is showing his impatience and is attempting to train you, rather than the other way round. He believes he can change a situation simply by making a noise – and even if he does not get what he wants any quicker, he is enjoying all the fuss as you shout at him to tell him to be quiet. He is still getting attention, so why inhibit his behaviour?

In this situation, the best and most effective response is to ignore your Pug. Do not talk to your Pug, and, most importantly, do not give him eye contact. Look in the opposite direction and wait until your Pug is calm and quiet. Then, and only then, should you talk to him and give him the attention he craves.

Repeat this on every occasion when your Pug barks for attention and he will soon learn that barking is non-productive. He is not rewarded by being lifted on to the sofa for a cuddle; in fact, it is even worse because he is not getting any attention at all. It will not take long for a clever Pug to realise that being quiet is the most effective strategy. In this scenario, you have not only taught your Pug that he must be quiet to get your attention, you have also earned his respect because you have taken control of the situation.

Stopping bad behaviour: There are occasions when you want to call an instant halt to whatever it is your Pug is doing. Pugs are great opportunists, and many will have a go at raiding the bin in the hope of finding a tasty snack. In this situation, your Pug has already committed the 'crime', so your aim is to stop him and to redirect his attention. You can do this by using a deep, firm tone of voice to say "No", which will startle him, and then call him to you in a bright, happy voice. If necessary, you can attract him with a toy or a treat. The moment your Pug stops the undesirable behaviour and comes towards you, you can reward his good behaviour. You can back this up by running through a couple of simple exercises, such as a 'Sit' or a 'Down', and rewarding with treats. In this way, your Pug focuses his attention on you and sees you as the greatest source of reward and pleasure.

In a more extreme situation, when you want to interrupt undesirable behaviour and you know that a simple "No" will not do the trick, you can try something a little more dramatic. If you get a can and fill it with

Caught red-handed! There are times when you need to call an instant halt to your Pug's behaviour.

pebbles, it will make a really loud noise when you shake it or throw it. The same effect can be achieved with purpose-made training discs. The dog will be startled and stop what he is doing. Even better, the dog will not associate the unpleasant noise with you. This gives you the perfect opportunity to be the nice guy, calling the dog to you and giving him lots of praise.

PROBLEM BEHAVIOUR

If you have trained your Pug from puppyhood, survived his adolescence and established yourself as a fair and consistent leader, you will end up with an outstanding companion dog. The Pug is a well-balanced dog, who rarely has hang-ups if he has been correctly reared and socialised.

However, you may have struggled to establish your role as leader, or it may be that you have taken on a rescued Pug that has established behavioural problems. If you are worried about your Pug and feel out of your depth, do not delay in seeking professional help. This is readily available, usually through a referral from your vet, or you can find additional information on the internet (see Appendices for web addresses). An animal behaviourist will have experience in tackling problem behaviour and will be able to help both you and your dog.

RESOURCE GUARDING

If you have trained and socialised your Pug correctly, he will know his place in the family pack and will have no desire to challenge your authority. But a Pug who does not respect his human family will become increasingly assertive. This behaviour can be expressed in many different ways, which may include the following:

• Showing lack of respect for your personal space. For example, your dog might run through doors ahead of you or jump up at you.
• Ignoring basic obedience commands.
• Showing no respect to younger members of the family.
• Male dogs may start marking (cocking their leg) in the house.
• Aggression towards people or other dogs (see page 103).

However, the most common behaviour displayed by a Pug who has ideas above his station, is resource guarding. This may take a number of different forms:

• Getting up on to the sofa or your favourite armchair and growling when you tell him to get back on the floor.
• Becoming possessive over a toy, or guarding his food bowl by growling when you get too close.
• Growling when anyone approaches his bed or where he is lying.

In each of these scenarios, the Pug has something he values and he aims to keep it. He does not have sufficient respect for you, his human leader, to give up what he wants and he is 'warning' you to keep away.

If you see signs of your Pug behaving in this way, you must work at lowering his status so that he realises that you are the leader and he must accept your authority. Although you need to be firm, you also need to use positive training methods so that your Pug is rewarded for the behaviour you want. In this way, his 'correct' behaviour will be strengthened and repeated.

The golden rule is not to become confrontational. The dog will see this as a challenge and may become even more determined not to co-operate. There are a number of steps you can take to lower your Pug's status, which are far more likely to have a successful outcome. They include:

• Go back to basics and hold daily training sessions. Make sure you have some really tasty treats, or find a toy your Pug really values and only bring it out at training sessions. Run through some of the training exercises you have taught your Pug. By giving him things to do, you are providing mental stimulation and you have the opportunity to make a big fuss of him and reward him when he does well. This will help to reinforce the message that you are the leader and that it is rewarding to do as you ask.
• Teach your Pug something new; this can be as simple as learning a trick, such as shaking paws. Having something new to think about will mentally stimulate your Pug and he will benefit from interacting with you.
• Be 100 per cent consistent with all house rules – your Pug must never sit on the sofa unless he is invited and you must never allow him to jump up at you.
• If your Pug is becoming possessive over toys, remove all his toys and keep them out of reach.

You may find your Pug becomes obsessed by a favourite toy and is reluctant to give it up.

It is then up to you to decide when to produce a toy and to initiate a game. Equally, it is you who will decide when the game is over and when to remove the toy. This teaches your Pug that you 'own' his toys. He has fun playing and interacting with you, but the game is over – and the toy is given up – when you say so.

- If your Pug is trying to 'guard' his food bowl, put the bowl down empty and drop in a little food at a time. Periodically stop dropping in the food and tell your Pug to "Sit" and "Wait". Give it a few seconds and then reward him by dropping in more food. This shows your Pug that you are the provider of the food and he can only eat when you allow him to.
- Make sure the family eats before you feed your Pug. Some trainers advocate eating in front of the dog (maybe just a few bites from a biscuit) before starting a training session, so the dog appreciates your elevated status.
- Do not let your Pug run through doors ahead of you or leap from the back of the car before you release him. You may need to put your dog on the lead and teach him to "Wait" at doorways and then reward him for letting you go through first.

If your Pug is progressing well with his retraining programme, think about getting involved with some extra curricular activities, such as the Good Citizen Scheme, or having a go at agility. This will give your Pug a positive outlet for his energies. However, if your Pug is still seeking to be dominant, or you have any other concerns, do not delay in seeking the help of an animal behaviourist.

SEPARATION ANXIETY

A Pug loves to be with people, but he must be brought up to accept short periods of separation from his owner so that he does not become anxious. A new puppy should be left for short periods on his own, ideally in a crate where he cannot get up to any mischief. It is a good idea to leave him with a boredom-busting toy so he will be happily occupied in your absence. When you return, do not rush to the crate and make a huge fuss. Wait a few minutes, and then calmly go to the crate and release your dog, telling him how good he has been. If this scenario is repeated a number of times, your Pug will soon learn that being left on his own is no big deal.

Problems with separation anxiety are most likely to arise if you take on a rescued dog who has major insecurities. You may also find your Pug hates being left if you have failed to accustom him to short periods of isolation when he was growing up. Separation anxiety is expressed in a number of ways and all are equally distressing for both dog and owner. An anxious dog who is left alone may bark and whine continuously, urinate and defecate, and may be extremely destructive.

There are a number of steps you can take when attempting to solve this problem.

- Put up a baby-gate between adjoining rooms and leave your dog in one room while you are in the other room. Your dog will be able to see you and hear you, but he is learning to cope without being right next to you. Build up the amount of time you can leave your dog in easy stages.
- Buy some boredom-busting toys and fill them with some tasty treats. Whenever you leave your dog, give him a food-filled toy so that he is busy while you are away.
- If you have not used a crate before, it is not too late to start. Make sure the crate is cosy and train your Pug to get used to going in his crate while you are in the same room. Gradually build up the amount of time he spends in the crate and then start leaving the room for short periods. Again, leave him with a boredom-busting toy, so that

If a Pug has not been brought up to accept periods on his own, he may become anxious.

he learns to associate time in his crate with good things. When you return, do not make a fuss of your dog. Leave him for five or ten minutes before releasing him, so that he gets used to your comings and goings.

- Pretend to go out, putting on your coat and jangling keys, but do not leave the house. An anxious dog often becomes hyped up by the ritual of leaving and this will help to desensitise him.

- When you go out, leave a radio or a TV on. Some dogs are comforted by hearing voices and background noise when they are left alone.

- Try to make your absences as short as possible when you are first training your dog to accept being on his own.

- If you take these steps, your dog should become less anxious, and, over a period of time, you should be able to solve the problem. However, if you find you are failing to make progress, do not delay in calling in expert help.

AGGRESSION

Aggression is a complex issue, as there are different causes and the behaviour may be triggered by numerous factors. It may be directed towards people, but far more commonly it is directed towards other dogs. Aggression in dogs may be the result of:

- Dominance (see page 100).
- Defensive behaviour: This may be induced by fear, pain or punishment.
- Territory: A dog may become aggressive if strange dogs or people enter his territory (which is generally seen as the house and garden).
- Intra-sexual issues: This is aggression between sexes – male-to-male or female-to-female.
- Parental instinct: A mother dog may become aggressive if she is protecting her puppies.

It is very rare for the Pug to show aggression in any shape or form. As we have seen, a warning growl from an over-assertive dog is pretty much a worst-case scenario. When interacting with other dogs, the Pug is generally calm and friendly, particularly if he meets them off-lead.

However, you may have taken on an older, rescued dog that has been poorly socialised and reacts to situations because he is wary. It is in a Pug's nature to relate to people, but a nervous dog may not read a person's intentions and become increasingly apprehensive. If he has had a bad experience with a bigger dog, he may react by being very submissive, or he may try to 'put on an act', particularly if he has the security of being on-lead.

If your Pug has been poorly socialised, he has missed out on a vital part of his education – but you can still make up for lost time. Take him out to meet lots of different people so that he learns to read human body language and understands he has nothing to fear. Work with other dogs of sound temperament in controlled situations so that he learns how to interact in a sensible manner.

However, if you are concerned about your dog's behaviour, you would be well advised to call in professional help. If the aggression is directed towards people, you should seek immediate advice. This behaviour can escalate very quickly and could lead to disastrous consequences.

NEW CHALLENGES

If you enjoy training your Pug you may want to try one of the many dog sports that are now on offer. A Pug is not going to hit the dizzy heights of success that you would expect from a Border Collie, for example, but you can have lots of fun having a go – and you never know, your Pug may surprise you.

GOOD CITIZEN SCHEME

This is a scheme run by the Kennel Club in the UK and the American Kennel Club in the USA. The schemes promote responsible ownership and helps you to train a well-behaved dog who will fit in with the community. The schemes are excellent for all pet owners and they are also a good starting point if you plan to compete with your Pug when he is older. The KC and the AKC schemes vary in format. In the UK there are four levels: foundation, bronze, silver and gold, with each test becoming progressively more demanding. In the AKC scheme there is a single test.

Some of the exercises include:
- Walking on a loose lead among people and other dogs.
- Recall amid distractions.

- A controlled greeting where dogs stay under control while their owners meet.
- The dog allows all-over grooming and handling by his owner, and also accepts being handled by the examiner.
- Stays, with the owner in sight and then out of sight.
- Food manners – allowing the owner to eat without begging and taking a treat on command.
- Sendaway – sending the dog to his bed.

The tests are designed to show the control you have over your

The Pug is more than capable of carrying out the exercises that are required in the Good Citizen scheme.

dog and his ability to respond correctly and remain calm in all situations. The Good Citizen Scheme is taught at most training clubs. For more information, log on to the Kennel Club or AKC website (see Appendices).

SHOWING

In your eyes, your Pug is the most beautiful dog in the world – but would a judge agree? Showing is a highly competitive sport and as the Pug becomes increasingly popular, classes are getting bigger. However, many owners get bitten by the showing bug, and their calendar is governed by the dates of the top showing fixtures.

To be successful in the show ring, a Pug must conform as closely as possible to the Breed Standard, which is a written blueprint describing the 'perfect' Pug (see Chapter Seven). To get started you need to buy a puppy that has show potential and then train him to perform in the ring. A Pug will be expected to stand in show pose, gait for the judge in order to show off his natural movement, and to be examined by the judge. This involves a detailed hands-on examination, so your Pug must be bombproof when handled by strangers.

Many training clubs hold ringcraft classes, which are run by experienced showgoers. At these classes, you will learn how to handle your Pug in the ring, and you will also find out about rules, procedures and show ring etiquette.

The best plan is to start off at

If you want to get involved in showing, your Pug must measure up to the Breed Standard.

some small, informal shows where you can practise and learn the tricks of the trade before graduating to bigger shows. It's a long haul starting in the very first puppy class, but the dream is to make your Pug into a Champion.

COMPETITIVE OBEDIENCE

In the UK, this sport is dominated by Border Collies, Working Sheepdogs, German Shepherd Dogs, and some of the gundog breeds, such as the Golden Retriever. However, in the USA, it is customary for a wide variety of breeds to take part, and a number of Pugs have made their mark.

There are various levels of achievement, but this is highly competitive even at the lower levels. Marks are lost for even the

slightest crooked angle noticed when the dog is sitting and if a dog has a momentary attention deficit or works too far away from his owner in heelwork, again points will be deducted.

The exercises that must be mastered include the following:

• Heelwork: Dog and handler must complete a set pattern on and off the lead, which includes left turns, right turns, about turns and changes of pace.
• Recall: This may be when the handler is stationary or on the move.
• Retrieve: This may be a dumbbell or any article chosen by the judge.
• Sendaway: The dog is sent to a designated spot and must go into an instant 'Down' until he

is recalled by the handler.
- Stays: The dog must stay in the 'Sit' and in the 'Down' for a set amount of time. In advanced classes, the handler is out of sight.
- Scent: The dog must retrieve a single cloth from a pre-arranged pattern of cloths that has his owner's scent, or, in advanced classes, the judge's scent. There may also be decoy cloths.
- Distance control: The dog must execute a series of moves ('Sit', 'Stand', 'Down') without moving from his position and with the handler at a distance.

Even though competitive obedience requires accuracy and precision, make it fun for your Pug, with lots of praise and rewards so that you motivate him to do his best. Many training clubs run advanced classes for those who want to compete in obedience, or you can hire the services of a professional trainer for one-on-one sessions.

AGILITY

This fun sport has grown enormously in popularity over the past few years, and the Pug has enjoyed a fair degree of success. If you fancy having a go, make sure you have good control over your Pug and keep him slim. Agility is a very physical sport, which demands fitness from both dog and handler.

In agility competitions, each dog must complete a set course over a series of obstacles, which include:
- Jumps (upright hurdles and long jump, varying in height – small, medium and large, depending on the size of the dog)
- Weaves
- A-frame
- Dog walk
- Seesaw
- Tunnels (collapsible and rigid)
- Tyre

Dogs may compete in Jumping classes, with jumps, tunnels and weaves, or in Agility classes,

If you work at motivation, a Pug can be successful in agility.

which have the full set of equipment. Faults are awarded for poles down on the jumps, missed contact points on the A-frame, dog walk and seesaw, and refusals. If a dog takes the wrong course, he is eliminated. The winner is the dog that completes the course in the fastest time with no faults. As you progress up the levels, courses become progressively harder with more twists, turns and changes of direction.

If you want to get involved in agility, you will need to find a club that specialises in the sport (see Appendices). You will not be allowed to start training until your Pug is 12 months old and you cannot compete until he is 18 months old. This rule is for the protection of the dog, who may suffer injury if he puts strain on bones and joints while he is still growing.

A Pug thrives on human company and if you spend quality time with your dog, he will become an outstanding companion.

DANCING WITH DOGS

This sport is relatively new, but it is becoming increasingly popular. It is very entertaining to watch, but it is certainly not as simple as it looks. To perform a choreographed routine to music with your Pug demands a huge amount of training.

Dancing with dogs is divided into two categories: Heelwork to Music and Canine Freestyle. In Heelwork to Music, the dog must work closely with his handler and show a variety of close 'heelwork' positions. In Canine Freestyle, the routine can be more flamboyant, with the dog working at a distance from the handler and performing spectacular tricks. Routines are judged on style and presentation, content and accuracy.

SUMMING UP

The Pug is one of the outstanding companion dogs in the world – and once you have owned one, no other breed will do. In fact, most Pug owners are not content with one, and soon become multi-dog households! The Pug is intelligent, fun-loving, mischievous and loyal – what more could you want? Make sure you keep your half of the bargain: spend time socialising and training your Pug so that you can be proud to take him anywhere and he will always be a credit to you.

THE PERFECT PUG

Chapter 7

Breeders of pedigree dogs have one goal in their sights – to breed the perfect specimen of their breed. Generation after generation is produced, with the hope of improving on some aspect, such as ear-set, dentition, movement, or coat colour. As well as appearance, health and temperament are of paramount importance, and breeders strive to produce sound, typical dogs that, in turn, will produce the next generation of sound, typical dogs.

WHAT IS A BREED STANDARD?

The bible for every breeder is the Breed Standard. This is a written description of the perfect breed specimen, originally drawn up by those responsible for developing the breed, with minor changes and modifications that have been

The Breed Standard is the bible of every breeder, judge and exhibitor.

The judge's task is to find the dog that conforms most closely to the Breed Standard.

made by specialists during the breed's history. The Breed Standard describes the perfect dog in detail, giving guidance of all points of conformation, coat, colour, movement and temperament. Breeders aspire to produce a dog that comes closest to matching this ideal – and it is this dog who will win honours in the show ring and will be used in future breeding programmes.

However, it is important to bear in mind the phrase "closest to the ideal", for despite the many great dogs that have been produced, there is no such thing as perfection. A dog may only have a minor fault, but, just as

SCALE OF POINTS

BRITISH SCALE OF POINTS

Head	10
Ears	5
Eyes	5
Moles	5
Wrinkles & Mask	10
Body	10
Neck	5
Coat	10
Colour	10
Trace	5
Legs & Feet	10
Tail	10
Symmetry & Size	5
TOTAL	100

AMERICAN SCALE OF POINTS

	FAWN	BLACK
Symmetry	10	10
Size	5	10
Condition	5	5
Body	10	10
Legs & Feet	5	5
Head	5	5
Muzzle	10	10
Ears	5	5
Eyes	10	10
Mask	5	--
Wrinkles	5	5
Tail	10	10
Trace	5	--
Coat	5	5
Colour	5	10
TOTAL	100	100

The judge will examine
each dog in turn.

After watching each Pug move, the judge must come to a decision.

HEALTH AND FITNESS FOR PURPOSE

In January 2009, the Kennel Club in the UK revised its Breed Standards and introduced the following clause, which is worthy of note: "A Breed Standard is the guideline which describes the ideal characteristics, temperament and appearance of a breed and ensures that the breed is fit for function. Absolute soundness is essential. Breeders and judges should at all times be careful to avoid obvious conditions or exaggerations which would be detrimental in any way to the health, welfare or soundness of this breed.

"From time to time, certain conditions or exaggerations may be considered to have the potential to affect dogs in some breeds adversely, and judges and breeders are requested to refer to the Kennel Club website for details of any such current issues. If a feature or quality is desirable it should only be present in the right measure."

A top winning Pug in the US: BISS Ch. Schoolhouse Pocket Watch.

with humans, it is impossible to produce a living creature that is free from faults.

Breeders and exhibitors also need to be aware that the Breed Standard is open to personal interpretation. A judge will assess every dog against the Breed Standard, but each judge will have a slightly different interpretation of the Breed Standard. For example, one judge may penalise a fault, such as ear-set, because, in his or her opinion, it affects a dog's expression, while another judge may be more concerned with the way a dog moves because this has a bearing on the overall conformation.

At one stage in the Pug's history, the Breed Standard was listed with points awarded to all the different portions of the Pug. This gave useful guidance as to what aspect of the Pug's appearance carried the most importance. The scale of points remained a part of the American Kennel Club Standard until 1991 when it was re-formatted in accordance with the AKC's request for consistency, and the scale of points was deleted. There are minor differences in the scale of points used in the UK and in the USA, but we can see that the overall picture is very much the same. Depending on where a dog show is held, the Breed Standard may vary slightly depending on the country's governing body. In the UK, the Breed Standard authorised by the Kennel Club is used, and, as this is where the breed was developed, the same Standard is used by the Federation Cynologique Internationale, which is the governing body for Europe and many other countries. In the USA, the Breed Standard is authorised by the American Kennel Club; it has minor differences in wording, but it is broadly similar to the Breed Standard used in the UK.

BREEDING SOUND, TYPICAL HEALTHY PUGS

The new addition to the Kennel Club Standard calls for "absolute soundness", but it is important to note that a judge cannot always assess "absolute soundness". One very famous judge said: "It is no good having absolute soundness if the dog is not typical of the breed". The head could be wrong, tail-set and carriage may not be typical; the eyes could be light and the ears incorrect.

However, the changes that have been made to the Pug Breed Standard are aimed at addressing potential health issues. These are highlighted in the analysis and interpretation given below. In the main, these refer to conditions associated with a brachycephalic breed. The short, broad muzzle and pushed-in nose can give rise to respiratory problems, and so moderation is called for, promoting health before cosmetic appearance. In fact, breathing problems seem to be more concerned with the soft palate than the flat face.

The only other health issue that seems to have become prevalent lately is hemivertebrae. This is a condition where certain vertebrae take on a different shape and cause paralysis by pressure on the spinal cord. However, reading back over old books and handbooks it would appear that this disorder has always existed, and it has only come to the fore recently because of the increased number of Pug puppies, resulting in a higher incidence of the condition. It is also important to bear in mind that hemivertebrae affects other breeds and is not confined to Pugs or to brachycephalic breeds.

A compact dog that is well proportioned and cobby in build.

113

'Multum in parvo' sums up the Pug's general appearance.

INTERPRETATION OF THE BREED STANDARD

GENERAL APPEARANCE
KC
Decidedly square and cobby, it is 'multum in parvo' shown in compactness of form, well knit proportions and hardness of muscle, but never to appear low on legs, nor lean and leggy.

AKC
Symmetry and general appearance are decidedly square and cobby. A lean, leggy Pug and a dog with short legs and a long body are equally objectionable. The Pug should be multum in parvo, and this condensation (if the word may be used) is shown by compactness of form, well-knit proportions, and hardness of developed muscle. Proportion square.

The proportion is certainly square – if the legs are too long or too short, then the proportions become a triangle.

A recent addition to the KC Standard states that the Pug should not appear low on his legs, neither should he appear lean or leggy.

CHARACTERISTICS/TEMPERAMENT
KC
Great charm, dignity and intelligence. Even-tempered, happy and lively disposition.

AKC
This is an even-tempered breed, exhibiting stability, playfulness, great charm, dignity, and an outgoing, loving disposition.

The temperament is usually very gentle and sweet, but full of fun. This is a dog that loves attention.

There is nothing in the KC Standard to show the temperament of the Pug – the description could almost apply to any breed of dog. The AKC Standard at least has a little more detail.

The Pug is a fascinating breed because dogs often show a mixture of traits. They can be naughty in a mischievous way and stubborn in training if they want to be. Equally, they are faithful and very loving and make excellent companions. They are very good and tolerant with children but can be a bit jealous of one another, though will rarely fight. They love to be the centre of attention and have soft toys to play with. Some will shake them, some will destroy them, and some will go to sleep with a portion of the toy in their mouth, sucking it or kneading it with their feet, rather like a puppy feeding.

HEAD AND SKULL
KC
Head relatively large and in proportion to body, round, not apple-headed, with no indentation of skull. Muzzle relatively short, blunt, square, not upfaced. Nose black, fairly large with well open nostrils. Wrinkles on forehead clearly defined without exaggeration. Eyes or nose never adversely affected or obscured by over nose wrinkle. Pinched nostrils and heavy over nose wrinkle is unacceptable and should be heavily penalised.

AKC
The head is large, massive, round – not apple-headed, with no indentation of the skull. The wrinkles are large and deep. The muzzle is short, blunt, square, but not upfaced.

The head should be large, round and fit into a square. The KC asks for a "relatively large" head, but it must be in proportion to the body. The AKC Standard goes a step further, using the description "massive", which could be a little misleading. The head on a male Pug should be larger than that of a female and the sex of the Pug should be immediately obvious from this. The top of the skull should be flat and show no signs of being apple-headed in either sex.

This is a brachycephalic breed and so is noted for having a short, broad muzzle. The Pug's muzzle should be shallow and wide, but it should not be upfaced, giving the appearance of

The head is large, contrasting with a short muzzle.

115

THE NOSE ROLL

A full nose roll: Judges in the UK may consider this a little too full as it could adversely affect the dog.

This Pug has a very moderate nose roll. Note the diamond marking on the head.

This nose roll is moderate, but still retains the typical Pug appearance.

a Bulldog. This will occur if the Pug is too strong in the lower jaw by being too undershot – which means the lower jaw protrudes past the upper jaw. A Pug that is too undershot in the jaw will show too much chin. The Pug should be slightly undershot but not show his teeth or his tongue. The muzzle should also be black and the upper lips should not be too long, which would give a rather miserable expression and look jowly.

Concern over health issues in the UK has resulted in an addition to this part of the Breed Standard. It now states: "Eyes or nose never adversely affected or obscured by over nose wrinkle. Pinched nostrils and heavy over nose wrinkle is unacceptable and should be heavily penalised." The aim is for breeders to produce a Pug without exaggeration in this department, and so a dog with a moderate nose roll and with wide nostrils should now be favoured. However, there is some debate over this issue. I had a Pug with a heavy over-nose wrinkle who lived to the ripe old age of 15 and suffered no breathing problems.

Pink noses show lack of pigment if permanent but occasionally this can occur if a bitch has been in season – in which case it will darken later.

The wrinkles on the forehead should be large and deep; they should be in the shape of a diamond, a shape that is made noticeable by the dark wrinkle marking on fawn dogs. Black Pugs also have the same markings, but they are, perhaps, not so obvious as on the fawns. There should also be a thumb mark or dark mark in the middle of the diamond on fawn Pugs. However, some Pugs are too pale on the forehead and really need more pigmentation in this area. If there is no pigmentation on the forehead, the wrinkles are more difficult to see.

EYES
KC
Dark, relatively large, round in shape, soft and solicitous in expression, very lustrous, and when excited, full of fire. Never protruding, exaggerated or showing white when looking straight ahead. Free from obvious eye problems.

AKC
The eyes are dark in color, very large, bold and prominent, globular in shape, soft and solicitous in expression, very lustrous, and, when excited, full of fire.

The eyes should be as dark as possible and positioned in line with the top of the nose. They should be large but not too prominent. Typically, the eyes should have a soft and solicitous expression when the Pug is relaxed, but they should be full of fire when a dog is excited. Amber

The eyes are large, lustrous and very expressive.

and orange-coloured eyes are incorrect.

Recent changes to the KC Breed Standard call for the eyes to be "relatively large and round in shape", whereas the wording in the previous Standard was "very large, globular in shape". It also adds that the eyes should not protrude, and not show white when the dog is looking straight ahead. The stated concern is that the eyes should be free from obvious health problems, which is something all breeders strive for. However, we do not want to go to the opposite extreme and produce a Pug that no longer looks like a Pug. Small eyes are untypical, although they seem to be getting more prevalent in the show ring today. This is a fault I would penalise, as I believe small eyes change the expression of the Pug. Some eyes are becoming so small they are barely visible and it is impossible to see the colour. The revised wording is "relatively large", and it is important that breeders and judges alike bear this in mind.

EARS
KC
Thin, small, soft like black velvet. Two kinds – 'Rose ear' – small drop-ear which folds over and back to reveal the burr. 'Button ear' – ear flap folding forward, tip lying close to skull to cover opening. Preference given to latter.

AKC
The ears are thin, small, soft, like black velvet. There are two kinds – the "rose" and the "button." Preference is given to the latter.

The ears are defined as either 'rose' or 'button'. Button ears are preferable; this type of ear should lie close to the head whereas the rose ear has a fold – like a pleat in the middle – but should not show the inside of the ear. Both types should be completely black and should feel thin and velvety. They should not be large but small and neat, and not reach below the level of the top of the eye. Some ears can be very large and reach well below the eye and often these are thicker and heavier. When the ears are too large, they appear to overpower the rest of the face, and can even make it look a different shape.

MOUTH
KC
Slightly undershot. Wide lower jaw with incisors almost in a

Button ears, which lie close to the head, are preferred.

straight line. Wry mouths, teeth or tongue showing all highly undesirable and should be heavily penalised.

AKC
A Pug's bite should be very slightly undershot.

In the section on Head and Skull, we have discussed the effect of a Pug that is too overshot. Both the KC and the AKC Standards make it clear that a jaw that is too overshot should be heavily penalised. A dog with this fault looks parrot-faced, the mouth giving the impression of a parrot's beak.

The KC Standard asks for a wide lower jaw, with the incisors almost in a straight line – this helps to give a wider muzzle.

Wry mouths are incorrect; this occurs when the upper and lower jaw are not exactly one above the other. This fault will inevitably see the tongue protruding on one side or other of the mouth.

NECK
KC
Slightly arched to resemble a crest, strong, thick with enough length to carry head proudly.

AKC
The neck is slightly arched. It is strong, thick, and with enough length to carry the head proudly.

The head should be carried on a neck that should have a crest or slight arch – this gives the carriage of the head a proud appearance. If the neck is too

The front legs are straight and set well under the body.

short, it gives a stuffy appearance whereby the head almost sits on the shoulders. Too short a neck could also possibly be the cause of breathing problems, as happens in people. Too long a neck makes a dog look very much like a camel.

FOREQUARTERS
KC
Legs very strong, straight, of moderate length, and well under body. Shoulders well sloped.

AKC
The legs are very strong, straight, of moderate length, and are set well under. The elbows should be directly under the withers when viewed from the side. The shoulders are moderately laid back. The pasterns are strong, neither steep nor down.

The front legs should be straight with plenty of bone and have firm pasterns; they should be set well apart to give a wide chest with plenty of heart and lung room. A dog with a narrow chest will lack this and should be faulted. Legs should be set well under the body.

The shoulders must have good angulation, as this will give correct front movement. If the shoulders are too upright or straight then the front movement will be incorrect, causing the legs to move with a 'hackney' gait.

This is caused by more angulation and drive from behind than in front. The dog resorts to extra-high action of the forelegs in order to keep the paws out of the way of the oncoming back feet. The term is taken from the hackney horse that exemplifies this action.

BODY
KC
Short and cobby, broad in chest. Ribs well sprung and carried well back. Topline level, neither roached nor dipping.

AKC
The short back is level from the withers to the high tail set. The body is short and cobby, wide in chest and well ribbed up.

The ribcage should be well rounded, as this gives more room for the lungs and other organs. In some Pugs, the ribs are not sufficiently rounded, which gives a slab-sided appearance.

The topline of the Pug should be level from the shoulders to the tail. Dipping at the shoulders is a fault, as it destroys the overall square, compact picture that we are looking for. Dipping at the shoulders seems to be becoming more and more prevalent in the breed today, and breeders should be careful that it does not begin to be accepted as the norm.

A roached back, where the topline rises in the middle of the back, is also undesirable. This conformational fault will often make the tail look low set.

It is important to eliminate these basic faults of conformation from breeding programmes, and breeders would do well to remember that breeding from two dogs with the same fault means it will almost certainly be prevalent in the offspring. Toplines can also be affected if a dog is too long from the pelvis to the hock.

The topline should be level from the shoulders to the tail.

HINDQUARTERS
KC
Legs very strong, of moderate length, with good turn of stifle, well under body, straight and parallel when viewed from rear.

AKC
The strong, powerful hindquarters have moderate bend of stifle and short hocks perpendicular to the ground. The legs are parallel when viewed from behind. The hindquarters are in balance with the forequarters. The thighs and buttocks are full and muscular.

The hindquarters of the Pug should be strong and well rounded with good muscle; there should be a good bend of stifle and not too long a hock. A Pug that is too straight in the stifle can often have a slope down to the shoulder, which is incorrect; too much length of bone down to the stifle can cause the same fault.

The hocks should be parallel and should not turn inwards towards one another, as this is then 'cow-hocked' and the hocks are then too weak. The positioning of the front and back legs should be the same distance apart, so, when moving, the Pug does not single track like many dogs with a narrower type of body. The tracking can easily be seen if the pattern of the feet is shown in the snow or in soft sand, with the hind feet falling in the same line as the front feet.

FEET
KC
Neither so long as the foot of the hare, nor so round as that of the cat; well split up toes; the nails black.

AKC
The feet are neither so long as the foot of the hare, nor so round as that of the cat; well split-up toes, and the nails black. Dewclaws are generally removed.

Both the KC Standard and the AKC Standard stipulate that feet should not be as round as those on the cat, but not long as in a hare's foot. The toes should be well split up without being splayed. The pads should be quite thick and black with the middle two toes being slightly longer than the outer toes.

Nails should be black; white claws show lack of pigment. Some people say this is only 'cosmetic', but, in that case, any lack of pigment in other areas could be given the same 'excuse'.

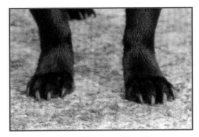

The toes should be well split without being splayed, and nails should be black.

Often the dewclaws are removed, as when the Pug has an irritable eye the front leg comes up to rub the eye and the dewclaw can then rake across it and scratch the cornea, resulting in an ulcer.

TAIL
KC
High-set, tightly curled over hip. Double curl highly desirable.

AKC
The tail is curled as tightly as possible over the hip. The double curl is perfection.

A single curl.

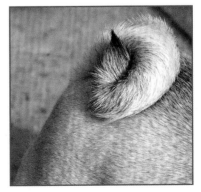

A double curl is preferred.

ASSESSING MOVEMENT

Viewed from the front, forelegs should be carried well forward.

A slight roll of the hindquarters when moving is a unique characteristic of the Pug.

The judge will also assess movement in profile.

Both the KC and AKC Standards are straightforward in their demand for a high-set, tightly curled tail. The KC Standard states a double curl is highly desirable, while the AKC Standard calls it "perfection'. In fact, judges will, first and foremost, look for a tight curl, making sure it curls right round the set (where the tail is 'set' on to the body). Some tails curl on the hips and some straight over the back.

GAIT/MOVEMENT

KC

Viewed from in front should rise and fall with legs well under shoulder, feet keeping directly to front, not turning in or out. From behind action just as true. Using forelegs strongly putting them well forward, with hind legs moving freely and using stifles well. A slight unexaggerated roll of hindquarters typifies gait. Capable of purposeful and steady movement.

AKC

Viewed from the front, the forelegs should be carried well forward, showing no weakness in the pasterns, the paws landing squarely with the central toes straight ahead. The rear action should be strong and free through hocks and stifles, with no twisting or turning in or out at the joints. The hind legs should follow in line with the front. There is a slight natural convergence of the limbs both fore and aft. A slight roll of the hindquarters typifies the gait which should be free, self-assured, and jaunty.

Correct movement in the Pug is a highly debated issue. The Pug is a double-tracking breed; the rear legs follow the front legs and a dog should never be gaited so quickly that it converges to the centre line of gravity, which often happens in the show ring.

The Pug's 'roll' is slight and does not compare with the Bulldog roll. This is because the Pug's roll comes from the front whereas the Bulldog's roll comes from the rear. Remember, this is a Toy breed, which means it was bred for enjoyment and companionship. A dog should, therefore, be gaited near the handler's side and not run around the ring on a six-foot lead.

COAT

KC

Fine, smooth, soft, short and glossy, neither harsh, off-standing nor woolly.

AKC

The coat is fine, smooth, soft, short and glossy, neither hard nor woolly.

The fawn-coloured Pug has a double coat with a soft undercoat and a fine, smooth, shiny outer coat. The coat should not be long or coarse.

The black Pug should have a fine, short single coat and not a double coat, as the fawn has.

Sometimes blacks will have a double coat, which may be due to breeding the two colours together. As long as the black Pug coat is really black, and the coat is smooth and soft and in good condition, this is not usually penalised. If the coat is showing a rusty colour in places, or the coat is harsh and poor, the dog would be faulted.

The skin of the Pug should be loose, but you should not see folds along the back.

COLOUR

KC

Silver, apricot, fawn or black. Each clearly defined, to make contrast complete between colour, trace (black line extending from occiput to tail) and mask. Markings clearly defined. Muzzle or mask, ears, moles on cheeks, thumb mark or diamond on forehead and trace as black as possible.

AKC

The colors are fawn or black. The fawn color should be decided so as to make the contrast complete between the color and the trace and mask. The markings are clearly defined. The muzzle or mask, ears, moles on cheeks, thumb mark or diamond on forehead, and the back trace should be as black as possible. The mask should be black. The more intense and well defined it is, the better. The trace is a black line extending from the occiput to the tail.

The black Pug should be pure black, with no white hairs on the chest.

There should be a clear contrast between the fawn coat colour and the black markings.

Coat colours of the Pug are either silver or apricot fawn, or black. The AKC Standard limits its description to "fawn", but the KC Standard gives more detail, describing the range of shades that are acceptable. The silver fawn is best described as a greyish fawn, but must not be confused with a smutty coat colour, which is incorrect. The apricot fawn is a warm colour; it should be quite a delicate shade or a light golden hue. The apricot is shaded, where the colour under the body and down the legs is a lighter shade.

Both Standards have detailed requirements for markings on fawn dogs. The trace, which is a black line about half-an-inch (1.25 cm) wide (which runs from the base of the skull to the tail) is not often seen nowadays. The width of the trace is important – it should not be like a dark saddle over the shoulders, or a wide, dark patch running along the back.

The black coat should be absolutely black, not showing a brownish tinge, and should not have any white hairs, which are sometimes seen on the chest.

Some colours are creeping into the fawn Pugs, which are quite peculiar. I have seen dogs that are so dark as to be more tan in colour. This colour looks quite odd in a line-up of true fawns. Overseas, there have been reports of some very odd colours that are trying to creep into the breed. One colour is a brindle, which has been shown abroad but has not been seen in the ring in this country as yet. The other colour is white. Some Pugs are getting almost too pale, but they tend to attract attention, as they look glamorous.

A change was made to the AKC Breed Standard in 2008 in relation to colour, as a number of brindle Pugs were starting to be shown, and some blue and white Pugs were being advertised.

SIZE
KC
Ideal weight 6.3-8.1 kgs (14-18 lbs). Should be hard of muscle but substance must not be confused with overweight.

AKC
Weight from 14 to 18 pounds (dog or bitch) desirable.

Both the KC Standard and the AKC Standard give a size guide in weight rather than height, and it is the same for males and females. The Standard asks for dogs to be up to 8.1 kgs (18 lbs) but many Pugs, especially the males, are heavier than this. In my view, it better to have a dog a little larger than the weight limit stipulated in the Breed Standard than a weedy type of Pug that is nearer the Standard weight. Having said this, we must bear in mind that this is a Toy dog, and too big a Pug is not correct. Pugs are usually very good eaters, so it is important to keep a close check on weight so dogs are not allowed to become fat.

FAULTS
KC
Any departure from the foregoing points should be considered a fault and the seriousness with which the fault should be regarded should

The guidelines for size are given in weight rather than height.

be in exact proportion to its degree and its effect upon the health and welfare of the dog. Note: Male animals should have two apparently normal testicles fully descended into the scrotum.

AKC
DISQUALIFICATION: Any color other than fawn or black

SUMMARY
There are some faults in Pugs that need to be addressed, namely hemivertebrae, slipping patellas and cleft palates. Hemivertebrae has been a problem in the breed for many years – there is written evidence from a breeder many years ago, who stated that she had Pugs with paralysis. However, all faults become more prevalent when more of the breed is produced. Pug breeding is at an all-time high, and, unfortunately, new breeders tend not to research pedigrees thoroughly and cannot be certain of the faults – or attributes – in dogs going back over a number of generations.

In my experience, nose rolls do not affect breathing, but they do not look attractive and can spoil the facial expression. Large eyes, though not prominent, give the true expression of a Pug. Some Pugs are now being bred with such small, squinting eyes that their colour cannot be seen unless the lids are opened. This gives completely the wrong expression – and it is the expression that comes from the eyes that is so very important.

The width of the bottom jaw is significant in creating the true face of a Pug. If a dog has too much chin, the expression is altered by giving a Bulldog look.

Attempts to change the Pug Breed Standard in too many ways will spoil the breed that we all know and love. Responsible breeders strive to produce, sound, healthy dogs that are typical of the breed. This must be our considered aim, making changes to improve health and wellbeing, but not robbing a breed of all its unique characteristics.

HAPPY AND HEALTHY

Chapter 8

Pugs are stoical dogs with a life span that can run well into double figures. Although classified as a Toy breed, bred as a house-dog, the Pug has a huge personality and will be a faithful companion and willing friend on a non-conditional basis. He will, however, of necessity rely on you for food and shelter, accident prevention and medication. Above all, a healthy Pug is a happy chap.

There are a few significant genetic conditions that have been recognised in the Pug, which will be covered in depth later in the chapter.

VACCINATION

There is much debate over the issue of vaccination at the moment. The timing of the final part of the initial vaccination course for a puppy and the frequency of subsequent booster vaccinations are both under scrutiny. An evaluation of the relative risk for each disease plays a part, depending on the local situation.

Many owners think that the actual vaccination is the protection, so that their puppy can go out for walks as soon as he or she has had the final part of the puppy vaccination course. This is not the case. The rationale behind vaccination is to stimulate the immune system into producing protective antibodies, which will be triggered if the patient is subsequently exposed to that particular disease. This means that a further one or two weeks will have to pass before an effective level of protection will have developed.

Vaccines against viruses stimulate longer-lasting protection than those against bacteria, whose effect may only persist for a matter of months in some cases. There is also the possibility of an individual failing to mount a full immune response to a vaccination: although the vaccine schedule may have been followed as recommended, that particular dog remains vulnerable.

A dog's level of protection against rabies, as demonstrated by the antibody titre in a blood sample, is routinely tested in the UK in order to fulfil the requirements of the Pet Travel Scheme (PETS). This is not required at the current time with any other individual diseases in order to gauge the need for booster vaccination or to determine the effect of a course of vaccines; instead, your veterinary surgeon will advise a protocol based upon the vaccines available, local disease prevalence, and the lifestyle of you and your dog.

It is worth remembering that

maintaining a fully effective level of immune protection against the disease appropriate to your locale is vital: these are serious diseases, which may result in the death of your dog, and some may have the potential to be passed on to his human family (so-called zoonotic potential for transmission). This is where you will be grateful for your veterinary surgeon's own knowledge and advice.

The American Animal Hospital Association laid down guidance at the end of 2006 for the vaccination of dogs in North America. Core diseases were defined as distemper, adenovirus, parvovirus and rabies. So-called non-core diseases are kennel cough, Lyme disease and leptospirosis. A decision to vaccinate against one or more non-core diseases will be based on an individual's level of risk, determined on lifestyle and where you live in the US.

Do remember, however, that the booster visit to the veterinary surgery is not 'just' for a booster. I am regularly correcting my

The annual booster provides an ideal opportunity to give your Pug an MOT.

clients when they announce that they have 'just' brought their pet for a booster. Instead, this appointment is a chance for a full health check and evaluation of how a particular dog is doing. After all, we are all conversant with the adage that a human year is equivalent to seven canine years.

There have been attempts in recent times to reset the scale for two reasons: small breeds live longer than giant breeds, and dogs are living longer than previously. I have seen dogs of 17 and 18 years of age, but to say a dog is 119 or 126 years old is plainly meaningless. It does emphasise the fact, though, that a dog's health can change dramatically over the course of a single year, because dogs age at a far faster rate than humans.

For me as a veterinary surgeon, the booster vaccination visit is a challenge: how much can I find of which the owner was unaware, such as rotten teeth or a heart murmur? Even monitoring bodyweight year upon year is of use, because bodyweight can creep up, or down, without an owner realising. Being overweight is unhealthy, but it may take an outsider's remark to make an owner realise that there is a problem. Conversely, a drop in bodyweight may be the only pointer to an underlying problem.

The diseases against which dogs are vaccinated include:

Kennel cough is highly infectious and will spread rapidly among dogs that live together.

ADENOVIRUS

Canine adenovirus 1 (CAV-1) affects the liver (hepatitis) and is seen within affected dogs as the classic 'blue eye', while CAV-2 is a cause of kennel cough (see later). Vaccines often include both canine adenoviruses.

DISTEMPER

This disease is sometimes called 'hardpad' from the characteristic changes to the pads of the paws. It has a worldwide distribution, but fortunately vaccination has been very effective at reducing its occurrence. It is caused by a virus and affects the respiratory, gastro-intestinal (gut) and nervous systems, so it causes a wide range of illnesses. Fox and urban stray dog populations are most at risk and are usually responsible for local outbreaks.

KENNEL COUGH

Also known as **infectious tracheobronchitis,** *Bordetella bronchiseptica* is not only a major cause of kennel cough but also a common secondary infection on top of another cause. Being a bacterium, it is susceptible to treatment with appropriate antibiotics, but the immunity stimulated by the vaccine is therefore short-lived (six to 12 months).

This vaccine is often in a form to be administered down the nostrils in order to stimulate local immunity at the point of entry, so to speak. Do not be alarmed to see your veterinary surgeon using a needle and syringe to draw up the vaccine, because the needle will be replaced with a special plastic introducer, allowing the vaccine to be gently instilled into each nostril. Dogs generally resent being held more than the actual intra-nasal vaccine, and I have learnt that covering the patient's eyes helps greatly.

Kennel cough is, however, rather a catch-all term for any cough spreading within a dog population – not just in kennels, but also between dogs at a training session or breed show, or even mixing in the park. Many of these infections may not be *B. bronchiseptica* but other viruses, for which one can only treat symptomatically. **Parainfluenza** virus is often included in a vaccine programme, as it is a common viral cause of kennel cough.

Kennel cough can seem alarming. There is a persistent cough accompanied by the

LEPTOSPIROSIS

This disease is caused by *Leptospira interogans*, a spiral-shaped bacterium. There are several natural variants or serovars. Each is characteristically found in one or more particular host animal species, which then acts as a reservoir, intermittently shedding leptospires in the urine. Infection can also be picked up at mating, via bite wounds, across the placenta, or through eating the carcases of infected animals (such as rats).

A serovar will cause actual clinical disease in an individual when two conditions are fulfilled: the individual is not the natural host species, and is also not immune to that particular serovar.

Leptospirosis is a zoonotic disease, known as Weil's disease in humans, with implications for all those in contact with an affected dog. It is also commonly called rat jaundice, reflecting the rat's important role as a carrier. The UK National Rodent Survey 2003 found a wild brown rat population of 60 million, equivalent at the time to one rat per person. Wherever you live in the UK, rats are endemic, which means that there is as much a risk to the Pug living with a family in a town as the Pug leading a more rural lifestyle.

Signs of illness reflect the organs affected by a particular serovar. In humans, there may be a flu-like illness or a more serious, often life-threatening disorder involving major body organs. The illness in a susceptible dog may be mild, the dog recovering within two to three weeks without treatment but going on to develop long-term liver or kidney disease. In contrast, peracute illness may result in a rapid deterioration and death following an initial malaise and fever. There may also be anorexia, vomiting, diarrhoea, abdominal pain, joint pain, increased thirst and urination rate, jaundice, and ocular changes. Haemorrhage is also a common feature, manifesting as bleeding under the skin, nosebleeds, and the presence of blood in the urine and faeces.

Treatment requires rigorous intravenous fluid therapy to support the kidneys. Being a bacterial infection, it is possible to treat leptospirosis with specific antibiotics, although a prolonged course of several weeks is needed. Strict hygiene and barrier nursing are required in order to avoid onward transmission of the disease.

Annual vaccination is recommended for leptospirosis because the immunity only lasts for a year, unlike the longer immunity associated with vaccines against viruses. There is, however, little or no cross-protection between Leptospira serovars, so vaccination will result in protection against only those serovars included in the particular vaccine used. Additionally, although vaccination against leptospirosis will prevent active disease if an individual is exposed to a serovar included in the vaccine, it cannot prevent that individual from being infected and becoming a carrier in the long-term.

In the UK, vaccines have classically included *L. icterohaemorrhagiae* (rat-adapted serovar) and *L. canicola* (dog-specific serovar). The latter is of especial significance to us humans, since disease will not be apparent in an infected dog but leptospires will be shed intermittently.

The situation in America is less clear-cut. Blanket vaccination against leptospirosis is not considered necessary, because it only occurs in certain areas. There has also been a shift in the serovars implicated in clinical disease, reflecting the effectiveness of vaccination and the migration of wildlife reservoirs carrying different serovars from rural areas, so you must be guided by your veterinarian's knowledge of the local situation.

production of white frothy spittle, which can last for a matter of weeks; during this time the patient is highly infectious to other dogs. I remember when it ran through our five Border Collies – there were white patches of froth on the floor wherever you looked! Other features include sneezing, a runny nose, and eyes sore with conjunctivitis. Fortunately, these infections are generally self-limiting, most dogs recovering without any long-lasting problems, but an elderly dog may be knocked sideways by it, akin to the effects of a common cold on a frail, elderly person.

LYME DISEASE

This is a bacterial infection transmitted by hard ticks. It is restricted to those specific areas of the US where ticks are found, such as the north-eastern states, some southern states, California and the upper Mississippi region. It does also occur in the UK, but at a low level, so vaccination is not routinely offered.

Clinical disease is manifested primarily as limping due to arthritis, but other organs affected include the heart, kidneys and nervous system. It is readily treatable with appropriate antibiotics, once diagnosed, but the causal bacterium, *Borrelia burgdorferi*, is not cleared from the body totally and will persist.

Prevention requires both vaccination and tick control, especially as there are other diseases transmitted by ticks. Ticks carrying *B. burgdorferi* will transmit it to humans as well, but an infected dog cannot pass it to a human.

PARVOVIRUS (CPV)

Canine parvovirus disease first appeared in the late 1970s, when it was feared that the UK's dog population would be decimated by it because of the lack of immunity in the general canine population. While this was a terrifying possibility at the time, fortunately it did not happen.

There are two forms of the virus (CPV-1, CPV-2) affecting domesticated dogs. It is highly contagious, picked up via the mouth/nose from infected faeces. The incubation period is about five days. CPV-2 causes two types of illness: gastro-enteritis and heart disease in puppies born to unvaccinated dams, both of which often result in death. Infection of puppies under three weeks of age with CPV-1 manifests as diarrhoea, vomiting, difficulty breathing, and fading

Fortunately, Lyme disease is still relatively rare in the UK.

RABIES

This is another zoonotic disease and there are very strict control measures in place. Vaccines were once available in the UK only on an individual basis for dogs being taken abroad. Pets travelling into the UK had to serve six months' compulsory quarantine so that any pet incubating rabies would be identified before release back into the general population. Under the Pet Travel Scheme (PETS), provided certain criteria are met (check the DEFRA website for up-to-date information – www.defra.gov.uk) then dogs can re-enter the UK without being quarantined.

Dogs to be imported into the US have to show that they were vaccinated against rabies at least 30 days previously; otherwise, they have to serve effective internal quarantine for 30 days from the date of vaccination against rabies, in order to ensure they are not incubating rabies. The exception is dogs entering from countries recognised as being rabies-free, in which case it has to be proved that they lived in that country for at least six months beforehand.

puppy syndrome. CPV-1 can cause abortion and foetal abnormalities in breeding bitches.

Occurrence is mainly low now, thanks to vaccination, although a recent outbreak in my area did claim the lives of several puppies and dogs. It is also occasionally seen in the elderly unvaccinated dog.

PARASITES

A parasite is defined as an organism deriving benefit on a one-way basis from another, the host. It goes without saying that it is not to the parasite's advantage to harm the host to such an extent that the benefit is lost, especially if it results in the death of the host. This means a dog could harbour parasites, internal and/or external, without there being any signs apparent to the owner. Many canine parasites can, however, transfer to humans with variable consequences, so routine preventative treatment is advised against particular parasites.

Just as with vaccination, risk assessment plays a part – for example, there is no need for routine heartworm treatment in the UK (at present), but it is vital in the US and in Mediterranean countries.

ROUNDWORMS (NEMATODES)

These are the spaghetti-like worms that you may have seen passed in faeces or brought up in vomit. Most of the deworming treatments in use today cause the adult roundworms to disintegrate, thankfully, so that treating puppies in particular is not as unpleasant as it used to be!

Most puppies will have a worm burden, mainly of a particular roundworm species (*Toxocara canis*), which reactivates within the dam's tissues during pregnancy and passes to the foetuses developing in the womb. It is therefore important to treat the dam both during and after pregnancy, as well as the puppies.

Professional advice is to continue worming every one to three months. There are roundworm eggs in the environment and, unless you examine your dog's faeces under a microscope on a very regular basis for the presence of roundworm eggs, you will be unaware of your dog having picked up roundworms, unless he should have such a heavy burden that he passes the adults.

It takes a few weeks from the time that a dog swallows a *Toxocara canis* roundworm egg to himself passing viable eggs (the pre-patent period). These eggs are not immediately infective to other animals, requiring a period of maturation in the environment, which is primarily temperature-dependent and therefore shorter in the summer (as little as two weeks) than in the winter. The eggs can survive in the environment for two years and more.

There are deworming products that are active all the time, which will provide continuous protection when administered as often as directed. Otherwise, treating every month will, in effect, cut in before a dog could theoretically become a source of roundworm eggs to the general population.

It is the risk to human health that is so important: *T. canis* roundworms will migrate within our tissues and cause all manner of problems, not least of which (but fortunately rarely) is blindness. If a dog has

It is important to continue the worming programme started by your puppy's breeder.

roundworms, the eggs also find their way on to his coat where they can be picked up during stroking. Sensible hygiene is therefore important. You should always carefully pick up your dog's faeces and dispose of them appropriately, thereby preventing the maturation of any eggs present in the fresh faeces.

TAPEWORMS (CESTODES)
When considering the general dog population, the primary source of the commonest tapeworm species will be fleas, which can carry the eggs. Most multi-wormers will be active against these tapeworms. They are not a threat to human health, but it is unpleasant to see the wriggly ricegrain tapeworm segments emerging from your dog's back passage while he is lying in front of the fire, and usually when you have guests for dinner!

A tapeworm of significance to human health is **Echinococcus granulosus**, found in a few parts of the UK, mainly in Wales. Man is an intermediate host for this tapeworm, along with sheep, cattle and pigs. Inadvertent ingestion of eggs passed in the faeces of an infected dog is followed by the development of so-called hydatid cysts in major organs, such as the lungs and liver, necessitating surgical removal. Dogs become infected through eating raw meat containing hydatid cysts. Cooking will kill hydatid cysts, so avoid feeding raw meat and offal in areas of high risk.

There are specific requirements for treatment with praziquantel within 24 to 48 hours of return into the UK under the PETS. This is to prevent the introduction of

Echinococcus multilocularis, a tapeworm carried by foxes on mainland Europe, which is transmissible to humans, causing serious or even fatal liver disease.

FLEAS

There are several species of flea, which are not host-specific. A dog can be carrying cat and human fleas as well as dog fleas, but the same flea treatment will kill and/or control them all. It is also accepted that environmental control is a vital part of a flea control programme. This is because the adult flea is only on the animal for as long as it takes to have a blood meal and to breed; the remainder of the life cycle occurs in the house, car, caravan, shed…

There is a vast array of flea control products available, with various routes of administration: collar, powder, spray, 'spot-on', or oral.

Flea control needs to be applied to all pets in the house, regardless of whether they leave the house,. This is because fleas can be introduced into the home by other pets and their human owners. Discuss your specific flea control needs with your veterinary surgeon.

HEARTWORM (DIROFILARIA IMMITIS)

Heartworm infection has been diagnosed in dogs all over the world. There are two prerequisites: the presence of mosquitoes, and a warm, humid climate.

When a female mosquito bites an infected animal, it acquires *D. immitis* in its circulating form, as microfilariae. A warm environmental temperature is needed for these microfilariae to develop into the infective third-stage larvae (L3) within the mosquitoes, the so-called intermediate host. L3 larvae are then transmitted by the mosquito when it next bites a dog. Therefore, while heartworm infection is found in all parts of the United States, it is at differing levels. An occurrence in Alaska, for example, is probably a reflection of a visiting dog having previously picked up the infection elsewhere.

Heartworm infection is not currently a problem in the UK, except for those dogs contracting it while abroad without suitable preventative treatment. Global warming and its effect on the UK's climate, however, could change that.

It is a potentially life-threatening condition, with dogs of all breeds and ages being susceptible without preventative treatment. The larvae can grow to 14 inches within the right side of the heart, causing primarily signs of heart failure and, ultimately, liver and kidney damage. It can be treated but prevention is a better plan. In the US, regular blood tests for the presence of infection are advised, coupled with appropriate preventative measures, so I would advise liaison with your veterinary surgeon.

For dogs travelling to heartworm-endemic areas of the EU, such as the Mediterranean coast, preventative treatment should be started before leaving the UK and maintained during the visit. Again, this is best arranged with your veterinary surgeon.

MITES

There are five types of mite that can affect dogs:

Demodex canis: This mite is a normal inhabitant of canine hair follicles, passed from the bitch to her pups as they suckle. The development of actual skin disease or demodicosis depends on the individual. It is seen frequently around the time of puberty and after a bitch's first season, associated with hormonal changes. There may, however, be an inherited weakness in an individual's immune system, enabling multiplication of the mite.

The localised form consists of areas of fur loss without itchiness, generally around the face and on the forelimbs, and 90 per cent will recover without treatment. The other 10 per cent develop the juvenile-onset generalised form, of which half will recover spontaneously. The other half may be depressed, go off their food, and show signs of itchiness due to secondary bacterial skin infections.

Treatment may be prolonged over several months and consists of regular bathing with a specific miticidal shampoo, often clipping away fur to improve access to the skin, together with a suitable antibiotic by mouth. There is also now a licensed 'spot-on'

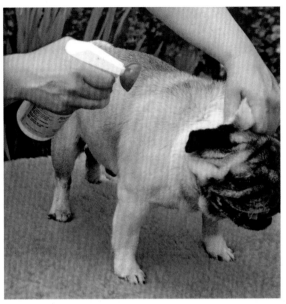

Preventative treatment in the form of a spray or spot-on treatment is effective in preventing infestation from fleas.

preparation available. Progress is monitored by the examination of deep skin scrapings for the presence of the mite; the initial diagnosis is based upon abnormally high numbers of the mite, often with live individuals being seen.

Some Pugs may develop the generalised form of demodicosis for the first time in middle-age (more than four years of age). This often reflects underlying immunosuppression by an internal disease, so it is important to identify such a cause and correct it where possible, as well as treating the skin condition.

Sarcoptes scabei: This characteristically causes an intense pruritus or itchiness in the affected Pug, making him incessantly scratch and bite at himself, leading to marked fur loss and skin trauma. Initially starting on the elbows, earflaps and hocks, without treatment the skin on the rest of the body can become affected, with thickening and pigmentation of the skin. Secondary bacterial infections are common.

Unlike *Demodex*, this mite lives at the skin surface, and it can be hard to find in skin scrapings. It is therefore not unusual to treat a patient for **sarcoptic mange (scabies)** based on the appearance of the problem even with negative skin scraping findings, and especially if there is a history of contact with foxes, which are a frequent source of the scabies mite.

It will spread between dogs and can therefore also be found in situations where large numbers of dogs from different backgrounds are mixing together. It will cause itchiness in humans, although the mite cannot complete its life cycle on us, so treating all affected dogs should be sufficient. Fortunately, there is now a highly effective 'spot-on' treatment for *Sarcoptes scabei*.

Cheyletiella yasguri: This is the fur mite most commonly found on dogs. It is often called 'walking dandruff' because it can be possible to see collections of the small white mite moving about over the skin surface. There is excessive scale and dandruff formation, and mild itchiness. It is transmissible to humans, causing a pruritic rash.

Diagnosis is by microscopic examination of skin scrapings, coat combings and sticky-tape impressions from the skin and fur. Treatment is with an appropriate insecticide, as advised by your vet.

Otodectes cynotis: A highly transmissible otitis externa (outer ear infection) results from the presence in the outer ear canal of this ear mite, characterised by exuberant

production of dark earwax. The patient will frequently shake his head and rub at the ear(s) affected. The mites can also spread on to the skin adjacent to the opening of the external ear canal, and may transfer elsewhere, such as to the paws.

When using an otoscope to examine the outer ear canal, the heat from the light source will often cause any ear mites present to start moving around. I often offer owners the chance to have a look, because it really is quite an extraordinary sight! It is also possible to identify the mite from earwax smeared on to a slide and examined under a microscope.

Cats are a common source of ear mites. It is not unusual to

find ear mites during the routine examination of puppies and kittens. Treatment options include specific eardrops acting against both the mite and any secondary infections present in the auditory canal, and certain 'spot-on' formulations. It is vital to treat all dogs and cats in the household to prevent recycling the mite between individuals.

(Neo-) Trombicula autumnalis: The free-living harvest mite can cause an intense local irritation on the skin. Its larvae are picked up from undergrowth, so they are characteristically found as a bright orange patch on the web of skin between the digits of the paws. It feeds on skin cells before

TICKS

Ticks have become an increasing problem in recent years throughout Britain. Their physical presence causes irritation, but it is their potential to spread disease that causes concern. A tick will transmit any infection previously contracted while feeding on an animal – for example, *Borrelia burgdorferi*, the causal agent of Lyme disease (see page 131).

The life cycle of the tick is curious: each life stage takes a year to develop and move on to the next. Long grass is a major habitat. The

vibration of animals moving through the grass will stimulate the larva, nymph or adult to climb up a blade of grass and wave its legs in the air as it 'quests' for a host on to which to latch for its next blood meal. Humans are as likely to be hosts, so ramblers and orienteers are advised to cover their legs when going through rough long grass.

Removing a tick is simple – provided your dog will stay still. The important rule is to twist gently so that the tick is persuaded to let go with its

dropping off to complete its life cycle in the environment.

Its name is a little misleading, because it is not restricted to the autumn nor to harvest-time; I find it on the earflaps of cats from late June onwards, depending on the prevailing weather. It will also bite humans.

Treatment depends on identifying and avoiding hotspots for picking up harvest mites, if possible. Checking the skin, especially the paws, after exercise and mechanically removing any mites found will reduce the chances of irritation, which can be treated symptomatically. Insecticides can also be applied – be guided by your veterinary surgeon.

A-Z OF COMMON AILMENTS

ANAL SACS, IMPACTED
The anal sacs lie on either side of the anus at approximately four and eight o'clock, if compared with the face of a clock. They fill with a particularly pungent fluid, which is emptied on to the faeces as they move past the sacs to exit from the anus. Theories abound as to why these sacs should become impacted periodically and seemingly more so in some dogs than others.

The irritation of impacted anal sacs is often seen as 'scooting', when the backside is dragged along the ground. Some dogs will also gnaw at their back feet or over the rump.

Increasing the fibre content of the diet helps some dogs; in others, there is underlying skin disease. It may be a one-off occurrence for no apparent reason. Sometimes an infection can become established, requiring antibiotic therapy, which may need to be coupled with flushing out the infected sac under sedation or general anaesthesia. More rarely, a dog will present with an apparently acute-onset anal sac abscess, which is incredibly painful.

DIARRHOEA
Cause and treatment much as Gastritis (see below).

Regular grooming will ensure you spot external parasites, such as ticks, at the earliest opportunity.

mouthparts. Grasp the body of the tick as near to your dog's skin as possible, either between thumb and fingers or with a specific tick-removing instrument, and then rotate in one direction until the tick comes away. I keep a plastic tick hook in my wallet at all times.

EAR INFECTIONS

The dog has a long external ear canal, initially vertical then horizontal, leading to the eardrum, which protects the middle ear. If your Pug is shaking his head, then his ears will need to be inspected with an auroscope by a veterinary surgeon in order to identify any cause, and to ensure the eardrum is intact. A sample may be taken from the canal to be examined under the microscope and cultured, to identify causal agents before prescribing appropriate eardrops containing antibiotic, antifungal agent and/or steroid. Predisposing causes of otitis externa or infection in the external ear canal include:

Cleaning the ears on a regular basis will reduce the risk of infection.

- Presence of a foreign body, such as a grass awn
- Ear mites, which are intensely irritating to the dog and stimulate the production of brown wax, predisposing to infection
- Previous infections, causing the canal's lining to thicken, narrowing the canal and reducing ventilation
- Bathing – take great care when bathing your Pug to avoid water entering the ears where it may become trapped and lead to infection. This is a concern in other breeds when swimming, but not usually for the Pug, who is not generally a keen swimmer!

FOREIGN BODIES

- **Internal:** Items swallowed in haste without checking whether they will be digested can cause problems if they lodge in the stomach or obstruct the intestines, necessitating surgical removal. Acute vomiting is the main sign. Common objects I have seen removed include stones from the garden, peach stones, babies' dummies, golf balls and, once, a lady's bra…

It is possible to diagnose a dog with an intestinal obstruction across a waiting room from a particularly 'tucked-up' stance and pained facial expression. These patients bounce back from surgery dramatically. A previously docile and compliant obstructed patient will return for a post-operative check-up and literally bounce into the consulting room.

- **External:** Grass awns are adept at finding their way into orifices such as a nostril, down an ear, and into the soft skin between two digits (toes), whence they start a one-way journey due to the direction of their whiskers. In particular, I remember a grass awn that migrated from a hindpaw, causing abscesses along the way but not yielding itself up until it erupted through the skin in the groin!

GASTRITIS

This is usually a simple stomach upset, most commonly in response to dietary indiscretion. Scavenging constitutes a change in the diet as much as an abrupt switch in the food being fed by the owner.

There are also some specific infections causing more severe gastritis/enteritis, which will require treatment from a veterinary surgeon (see also **Canine Parvovirus** under 'Vaccination' on page 131).

Generally, a day without food, followed by a few days of small, frequent meals of a bland diet (such as cooked chicken or fish), or an appropriate prescription diet, should allow the stomach to settle. It is vital to ensure the patient is drinking and retaining sufficient water to cover losses resulting from the stomach upset in addition to the normal losses to be expected when healthy. Oral rehydration fluid may not be very appetising for the patient, in which case cooled boiled water should be offered. Fluids should initially be offered in small but frequent amounts to avoid over-drinking, which can result in further vomiting and thereby dehydration and electrolyte imbalances. It is also important to wean the patient back on to routine food gradually or else another bout of gastritis may occur.

JOINT PROBLEMS

It is not unusual for older Pugs to be stiff after exercise, particularly in cold weather. This is not really surprising, given that they are such busy dogs when young. This is such a game breed that a nine- or ten-year-old Pug will not readily forego an extra walk or take kindly to turning for home earlier than usual. Your veterinary surgeon will be able to advise you on ways of helping your dog cope with stiffness, not least of which will be to ensure that he is not overweight. Arthritic joints do not need to be burdened with extra bodyweight!

LUMPS & BUMPS

Regularly handling and stroking your dog will enable the early detection of lumps and bumps. These may be due to infection (abscess), bruising, multiplication of particular cells from within the body, or even an external parasite (tick). If you are worried about any lump you find, have it checked by a veterinary surgeon.

OBESITY

Being overweight does predispose to many other problems, such as diabetes mellitus, heart disease and joint problems. It is so easily prevented by simply acting as your Pug's conscience. Ignore pleading eyes and feed according to your dog's waistline. The body condition is what matters qualitatively, alongside monitoring that individual's bodyweight as a quantitative measure. The Pug should, in my opinion as a health professional, have at least a suggestion of a waist and it should be possible to feel the ribs beneath only a slight layer of fat.

Neutering does not automatically mean that your Pug will be overweight. Having an ovario-hysterectomy does slow down the body's rate of working, castration to a lesser extent, but it therefore means that your dog needs less food. I recommend cutting back a little on the amount of food fed a few weeks before neutering to accustom your Pug to less food. If she

It is your responsibility to keep your Pug at the correct weight.

A routine of regular exercise plus feeding a well balanced diet will prevent problems with obesity.

looks a little underweight on the morning of the operation, it will help the veterinary surgeon as well as giving her a little leeway weight-wise afterwards. It is always harder to lose weight after neutering than before, because of this slowing in the body's inherent metabolic rate.

TEETH PROBLEMS

Eating food starts with the canine teeth gripping and killing prey in the wild, incisor teeth biting off pieces of food, and the molar teeth chewing it. To be able to eat is vital for life, yet the actual health of the teeth is often overlooked: unhealthy teeth can predispose to disease, and not just by reducing the ability to eat. The presence of infection within the mouth can lead to bacteria entering the bloodstream and then filtering out at major organs, with the potential for serious

consequences. That is not to forget that simply having dental pain can affect a dog's wellbeing, as anyone who has had toothache will confirm.

Veterinary dentistry has made huge leaps in recent years, so that it no longer consists of extraction as the treatment of necessity. Good dental health lies in the hands of the owner, starting from the moment the dog comes into your care. Just as we have taken on responsibility for feeding, so we have acquired the task of maintaining good dental and oral hygiene. In an ideal world, we should brush our dogs' teeth as regularly as our own. The Pug puppy who finds having his teeth brushed is a huge game and excuse to roll over and over on the ground requires loads of patience, twice a day.

There are alternative strategies, ranging from dental chewsticks to

specially formulated foods, but the main thing is to be aware of your dog's mouth. At least train your puppy to permit the full examination of his teeth. This will not only ensure you are checking in his mouth regularly but will also make your veterinary surgeon's job easier when there is a real need for your dog to 'open wide!'

INHERITED DISORDERS

Any individual, dog or human, may have an inherited disorder by virtue of the genes acquired from the parents. This is significant not only for the health of that individual but also because of the potential for transmitting the disorder on to that individual's offspring and to subsequent generations, depending on the mode of inheritance.

There are control schemes in

place for some inherited disorders. In the US, for example, the Canine Eye Registration Foundation (CERF) was set up by dog breeders concerned about heritable eye disease, and provides a database of dogs who have been examined by diplomates of the American College of Veterinary Ophthalmologists.

To date, only a few conditions have been confirmed in the Pug as being hereditary. In alphabetical order, these include:

BRACHYCEPHALIC UPPER AIRWAY SYNDROME
This is essentially an anatomical and conformational problem. A combination of pinched nostrils and a short, pushed-in face, and especially if coupled with an overlong soft palate, can lead to a reduced ability to cope with stresses such as hot weather and high humidity.

COLLAPSING TRACHEA
A malformation of the windpipe's rings of cartilage results in the airway collapsing, restricting airflow into the lungs. There is a characteristic honking cough, more often during the day because it is commonly precipitated by pressure on the neck (pulling against a collar, for example, so use of a harness is often advised), excitement, eating or drinking. Collapsing trachea can be a complicating factor in **brachycephalic upper airway syndrome** (see above).

ENTROPION
There is an inrolling of the eyelids, usually of the medial portion of the lower eyelids. There are degrees of entropion, ranging from a slight inrolling to the more serious case, requiring surgical correction because of the pain and damage to the surface of the eyeball. Polygenic inheritance is likely.

HEMIVERTEBRAE
The vertebrae are the building blocks of the bony spine, designed to protect the spinal cord as it runs from the underside of the brain down the

Responsible breeders screen all breeding stock to eliminate the risk of inherited disease.

It is the tear glands
that keep the eyes
properly lubricated.

length of the back through the canal enclosed within them. Hemivertebrae are misshapen, deformed vertebrae whose protective role is therefore compromised. Effects on the individual will be determined by the nature of the deformity, at worst resulting in paralysis. Surgery may be possible but needs careful pre-operative evaluation.

KERATOCONJUNCTIVITIS SICCA (KCS, dry eye)

Each eye is lubricated by tears produced by two tear glands, one within the eye socket and a smaller one associated with the third eyelid. KCS results when there is inadequate tear production by the glands (hence 'dry eye'), and is usually bilateral, affecting the tear glands in both eyes. It is characterised by a sore, red appearance to the eye with a thick ocular discharge and, ultimately, clouding of the cornea and loss of vision. The cause is generally unknown or inherited but, rarely, dry eye may result from trauma, infection, hypothyroidism or an adverse reaction to a drug.

Diagnosis is made with a Schirmer tear strip, which assesses the tear production in each eye. Surgical transposition of the parotid salivary duct was the favoured treatment, but medical therapy is now more often the therapy of choice, aimed at stimulating the underactive tear glands.

LEGGE-CALVE-PERTHES DISEASE

Also called Legge-Perthes disease, the problem is more accurately described as an avascular necrosis of the femoral head, meaning the ball of the thigh bone dies before skeletal maturity, resulting in severe pain and lameness apparent from a young age, typically in pups four to six months old. Surgery can be quite effective. Early diagnosis and treatment through pain relief and resting of the affected back-leg in a sling may avoid the need for surgical intervention.

HIP DYSPLASIA

Malformation of the hip joint results in pain, lameness and reduced exercise tolerance in the young Pug, resulting in degenerative joint disease (arthritis) in the older dog. Each hip joint is scored on several features to give a total of zero to 53 from a radiograph taken with the hips and pelvis in a specified position, usually requiring the dog to be sedated, after the age of one year under the British Veterinary Association/Kennel Club/International Sheep Dog Society Scheme, from two years of age in the US under the Orthopedic Foundation for Animals.

Just 20 individuals had been screened under the BVA/KC Scheme as of 1 November 2007, giving a mean score for both hips of 20 but a range of 8 to 53. Hip dysplasia is perceived as a major problem in the breed in the US.

PATELLAR LUXATION

This is the condition that I point out to my children when I spot a dog walking along the road, giving a little hop for a few steps every now and again. The kneecap or patella is slipping out of position, locking the knee or stifle so that it will not bend, causing the characteristic hopping steps until the patella slips back into its position over the stifle joint. Surgical correction is possible in severely affected dogs, but many simply carry on intermittently hopping, the long-term effect inevitably being arthritis of the stifle.

PUG DOG ENCEPHALITIS (PDE)

This is a rare, fatal inflammatory disease of the brain that occurs in the Pug. Sadly, diagnosis is based on *post mortem* examination of brain tissue. Clinical signs generally start as loss of vision, fits and circling, progressing to coma and death, often within the space of a few days or weeks.

Since it seems to run in certain lines, a genetic component is suspected. Age at onset is generally young, from six months, but may be as late as seven years, which could mean that an affected individual had been bred before developing signs of this distressing condition.

COMPLEMENTARY THERAPIES

Just as for human health, I do believe that there is a place for alternative therapies alongside and complementing orthodox treatment under the supervision of a veterinary surgeon. That is why 'complementary therapies' is a better name.

Because animals do not have a choice, there are measures in place to safeguard their wellbeing and welfare. All manipulative treatment must be under the direction of a veterinary surgeon who has examined the patient and diagnosed the condition that he or she feels needs that form of treatment. This covers **physiotherapy, chiropractic, osteopathy** and **swimming therapy**. For example, dogs with arthritis who cannot exercise as

Increasingly owners are becoming aware of the benefits of complementary therapies.

freely as they were accustomed will enjoy the sensation of controlled non-weight-bearing exercise in water, and will benefit from improved muscling and overall fitness.

All other complementary therapies, such as acupuncture, homoeopathy and aromatherapy, can only be carried out by veterinary surgeons who have been trained in that particular field. **Acupuncture** is mainly used in dogs for pain relief, often to good effect. The needles look more alarming to the owner, but they are very fine and are well tolerated by most canine patients. Speaking personally, superficial needling is not unpleasant and does help with pain relief.
Homoeopathy has had a mixed press in recent years. It is based on the concept of treating like with like. Additionally, a homoeopathic remedy is said to become more powerful the more it is diluted.

SUMMARY

As the owner of a Pug, you are responsible for his care and health. Not only must you make decisions on his behalf, you are also responsible for establishing a lifestyle for him that will ensure he leads a long and happy life. Diet plays an important part in this, as does exercise.

For the domestic dog, it is only in recent years that the need has been recognised for changing the diet to suit the dog as he grows, matures and then enters his twilight years. So-called life-stage diets try to match the nutritional needs of the dog as he progresses through life.

An adult dog food will suit the Pug living a standard family life. There are also foods for those

With good care and management, your Pug should live a long, happy and healthy life.

Pugs tactfully termed as obese-prone, such as those who have been neutered or are less active than others, or simply like their food. Do remember, though, that ultimately you are in control of your Pug's diet, unless he is able to profit from scavenging!

On the other hand, prescription diets are of necessity fed under the supervision of a veterinary surgeon because each is formulated to meet the very specific needs of a particular health condition. Should a prescription diet be fed to a healthy dog, or to a dog with a different illness, there could be adverse effects.

It is important to remember that your Pug has no choice. As his owner, you are responsible for any decision made, so it must be as informed a decision as possible. Always speak to your veterinary surgeon if you have any worries about your Pug. He is not just a dog: from the moment you brought him home, he became a member of the family.

THE CONTRIBUTORS

THE EDITOR: THE LATE NANCY TARBITT (NANCHYL)

The recent death of Nancy Tarbitt of the world-famous Nanchyl Pugs is a great loss to all those who love Pugs in Britain and abroad. For more than 40 years she bred and showed Pugs of the highest quality, including Champions such as Nanchyl Troglodite, Xerxes, Zechim, Roxanna and Rosalia to name but a few. In the process she won around 250 Challenge Certificates – a record that will be hard to equal.

During these years Nancy had many important wins at Crufts and elsewhere. They are too numerous to mention but I consider her most notable success to be her Best In Show win at the Pug Dog Club Centenary Show in 1983, in a then world-record entry, closely followed by the BIS wins of the beautiful Ch. Rosalia at Windsor and East of England All Breed Championship Shows in 1991.

Away from the show ring Nancy served the breed with great distinction and dedication, sitting on numerous committees. For many years she was Chairman of the Northern Pug Dog Club and the Breed Council.

Nancy was born in Yorkshire, where her family owned a number of farms around Malton. Her first love was horses, but while she was at school music took over. Her talent was such that at only 18 she was invited several times to play the organ at York Minster, and inevitably music became her career. Later, after her marriage and up until her death, she was a hugely popular piano teacher. I remember vividly that matings between her Pugs were often enlivened by music, with one of her pupils playing in the background.

Pugs came on the scene when she was exercising the family's elderly Dachshund in the park and they met up with a Pug. Instantly smitten, she vowed that when the time came their next dog had to be a Pug. It was, and within a comparatively short time she made up her first Champion, Patrick of Paramin, and the rest is history.

An indefatigable exhibitor, instantly recognisable in her lucky scarlet top, she will be much missed.
A tribute by Mary le Gallais (Gais Pugs)

MAUREEN P. WRIGHT (POLZEATH)

Maureen bought her first Pug more than 40 years ago, little knowing how much this would change the direction of her life. She first fell in love with the breed when she met a delightful Pug on a beach in Cornwall. It was not long after that she acquired her first Pug and was persuaded to show. Before long,

she hd registered her Polzeath affix with the Kennel Club and bred her first litter of Pugs in 1970.

From these beginnings, Maureen went on to breed several generations of show winning fawns, the most notable being Ch. Polzeath Forget Me Not. In recent years, Maureen has added blacks to her kennels.

Maureen has considerable all-round expereince in the breed and began to judge at Open level in 1975, progressing to awarding CCs in 1982. She has since judged at many Championship and Open shows in the UK and abroad.

Maureen continues to show a keen interest in breeding Pugs, particularly in the study of Pedigrees and the rearing and nursing of sick puppies. She says "Pugs and their welfare will always be at the core of my being and I cannot imagine a life without them."
See Chapter One: Getting to Know The Pug; Chapter Three: A Pug for your Lifestyle.

JIM TODD

Having been a Pug admirer from boyhood (an admiration shared by his wife Ann), it was not until Ann's retirement in 1982 that Jim and his wife acquired their first Pug – initially as a pet but the showing 'bug' soon bit.

Jim's involvement with the show world began as a chaiffeur and general dogsbody at dog shows, then in 1995, he was offered and accepted the post of Cup Steward for The Pug Dog Club. The history of these cups and their donors was of great personal interest - and sparked off the idea of regular articles in the club *Bulletin*, which ran from 1996 to 2003. A this point Jim accepted the post of Club Historian and was made an Honorary Life Member. With intensified research it has been possible to continue with regular historic *Bulletin* articles to the present day, which will hopefully contnue well into the future. Jim says "Whatever I can say or do to enhance the name 'Pug' is always paramount to me."
See Chapter Two: The First Pugs.
Special thanks are due to Jim Todd for casting a final editorial eye over this publication following the death of Nancy Tarbitt.

CHARLOTTE P. PATTERSON (IVANWOLD)

Charlotte purchased her first Pug in 1969. It was a pet but it began a love affair with the breed that has shaped her life. With her late husband, Edward, she has participated in the sport of dogs on many levels – breeder, exhibitor, professional handler and for the last 20 years, judging. The Pattersons also owned Pekes, Bostons, Yorkies, Cavaliers and

Whippets. Charlotte was a professional handler for over 10 years, campaigning three Pugs to the No.1 ranking in America for six years in a row. A Pug she bred won the Toy group at Westminster in 1980.

Charlotte is the current President of the Pug Dog Club of America, and is also the Show Chairman for the Okaloosa Kennel Club in Ft. Walton Beach, Florida and the Vice President of the Dog Judges Association of America. She was honoured to judge Pugs at Westminster and has also judged the National Specialty twice.
See Chapter Two: The Pug in North America.

JULIA BARNES

Julia has owned and trained a number of different dog breeds, and has also worked as a puppy socialiser for Dogs for the Disabled. A former journalist, she has written many books, including several on dog training and behaviour. Julia is indebted to Elaine Passmore for her specialist knowledge about Pugs.
See Chapter Six: Training and Socialisation.

ELAINE PASSMORE (PELANCY)

Elaine has lived with animals all her life and has worked with them for the last 30 years. She bought her first Pug at the age of 19 to go with German Shepherd-Collie cross. This experiment worked so well that Elaine has often kept a larger dog with her growing family of Pugs. Elaine bought her first show dog some 13 years ago and she has bred a number of both black and fawn litters under her Pelancy affix. Many of the puppies have now made their mark in the show ring. Elaine is a member of the three British Pug breed clubs and belongs to Wales and East of England Pug Dog Rescue.
See Chapter Six: Training and Socialisation.

ALISON LOGAN MA VetMB MRCVS

Alison qualified as a veterinary surgeon from Cambridge University in 1989, having been brought up surrounded by all manner of animals and birds in the north Essex countryside. She has been in practice in her home town ever since, living with her husband, two children and Labrador Retriever Pippin.

She contributes on a regular basis to *Veterinary Times, Veterinary Nurse Times, Dogs Today, Cat World* and *Pet Patter*, the PetPlan newsletter. In 1995, Alison won the Univet Literary Award with an article on Cushing's Disease, and she won it again (as the Vetoquinol Literary Award) in 2002, writing about common conditions in the Shar-Pei.
See Chapter Eight: Happy and Healthy.

USEFUL ADDRESSES

KENNEL & BREED CLUBS

UK
The Kennel Club
1 Clarges Street, London, W1J 8AB
Tel: 0870 606 6750
Fax: 0207 518 1058
Web: www.the-kennel-club.org.uk

To obtain up-to-date contact information for the following breed clubs, please contact the Kennel Club:
• Northern Pug Dog Club
• Pug Dog Club
• Scottish Pug Dog Club
• Wales & West of England Pug Dog Club
• West Pennine Pug Dog Club

USA
American Kennel Club (AKC)
5580 Centerview Drive,
Raleigh, NC 27606, USA.
Tel: 919 233 9767
Fax: 919 233 3627
Email: info@akc.org
Web: www.akc.org

United Kennel Club (UKC)
100 E Kilgore Rd, Kalamazoo,
MI 49002-5584, USA.
Tel: 269 343 9020
Fax: 269 343 7037
Web:www.ukcdogs.com/

Pug Dog Club of America, Inc.
Secretary, 449 Maar Avenue,
Fremont, CA 94536
Email: pugsrus2@comcast.net
Web: www.pugs.org/

For contact details of regional clubs, please contact the Pug Dog Club of America.

AUSTRALIA
Australian National Kennel Council (ANKC)
The Australian National Kennel Council is the administrative body for pure breed canine affairs in Australia. It does not, however, deal directly with dog exhibitors, breeders or judges. For information pertaining to breeders, clubs or shows, please contact the relevant State or Territory Controlling Body.

Dogs Australian Capital Teritory
PO Box 815, Dickson ACT 2602
Tel: (02) 6241 4404
Fax: (02) 6241 1129
Email: administrator@dogsact.org.au
Web: www.dogsact.org.au

Dogs New South Wales
PO Box 632, St Marys, NSW 1790
Tel: (02) 9834 3022 or 1300 728 022 (NSW Only)
Fax: (02) 9834 3872
Email: info@dogsnsw.org.au
Web: www.dogsnsw.org.au

Dogs Northern Territory
PO Box 37521, Winnellie NT 0821
Tel: (08) 8984 3570
Fax: (08) 8984 3409
Email: admin@dogsnt.com.au
Web: www.dogsnt.com.au

Dogs Queensland
PO Box 495, Fortitude Valley Qld 4006
Tel: (07) 3252 2661
Fax: (07) 3252 3864
Email: info@dogsqueensland.org.au
Web: www.dogsqueensland.org.au

Dogs South Australia
PO Box 844
Prospect East SA 5082
Tel: (08) 8349 4797
Fax: (08) 8262 5751
Email: info@dogssa.com.au
Web: www.dogssa.com.au

Tasmanian Canine Association Inc
The Rothman Building
PO Box 116
Glenorchy Tas 7010
Tel: (03) 6272 9443
Fax: (03) 6273 0844
Email: tca@iprimus.com.au
Web: www.tasdogs.com

Dogs Victoria
Locked Bag K9
Cranbourne VIC 3977
Tel: (03)9788 2500
Fax: (03) 9788 2599
Email: office@dogsvictoria.org.au
Web: www.dogsvictoria.org.au

Dogs Western Australia
PO Box 1404
Canning Vale WA 6970
Tel: (08) 9455 1188
Fax: (08) 9455 1190
Email: k9@dogswest.com
Web: www.dogswest.com

INTERNATIONAL
Fédération Cynologique Internationalé (FCI)/World Canine Organisation
Place Albert 1er, 13, B-6530 Thuin, Belgium.
Tel: +32 71 59.12.38
Fax: +32 71 59.22.29
Web: www.fci.be/

TRAINING AND BEHAVIOUR

UK
Association of Pet Dog Trainers
PO Box 17, Kempsford, GL7 4WZ
Telephone: 01285 810811
Email: APDToffice@aol.com
Web: http://www.apdt.co.uk

Association of Pet Behaviour Counsellors
PO BOX 46, Worcester, WR8 9YS
Telephone: 01386 751151
Fax: 01386 750743
Email: info@apbc.org.uk
Web: http://www.apbc.org.uk/

USA
Association of Pet Dog Trainers
101 North Main Street, Suite 610
Greenville, SC 29601, USA.
Tel: 1 800 738 3647
Email: information@apdt.com
Web: www.apdt.com/

American College of Veterinary Behaviorists
College of Veterinary Medicine, 4474 Tamu, Texas A&M University
College Station, Texas 77843-4474
Web: http://dacvb.org/

American Veterinary Society of Animal Behavior
Web: www.avsabonline.org/

AUSTRALIA

APDT Australia Inc
PO Box 3122, Bankstown Square, NSW 2200, Australia.
Email: secretary@apdt.com.au
Web: www.apdt.com.au

Canine Behaviour
For details of regional behvaiourists, contact the relevant State or Territory Controlling Body.

ACTIVITIES

UK
Agility Club
http://www.agilityclub.co.uk/

British Flyball Association
PO Box 990, Doncaster, DN1 9FY
Telephone: 01628 829623
Email: secretary@flyball.org.uk
Web: http://www.flyball.org.uk/

North American Dog Agility Council
P.O. Box 1206, Colbert,
OK 74733, USA.
Web: www.nadac.com/

North American Flyball Association, Inc.
1333 West Devon Avenue, #512
Chicago, IL 60660
Tel/Fax: 800 318 6312
Email: flyball@flyball.org
Web: www.flyball.org/

AUSTRALIA

Agility Dog Association of Australia
ADAA Secretary, PO Box 2212,
Gailes, QLD 4300, Australia.
Tel: 0423 138 914
Email: admin@adaa.com.au
Web: www.adaa.com.au/

NADAC Australia (North American Dog Agility Council - Australian Division)
12 Wellman Street, Box Hill South, Victoria 3128, Australia.
Email: shirlene@nadacaustralia.com
Web: www.nadacaustralia.com/

Australian Flyball Association
PO Box 4179, Pitt Town, NSW 2756
Tel: 0407 337 939
Email: info@flyball.org.au
Web: www.flyball.org.au/

INTERNATIONAL

World Canine Freestyle Organisation
P.O. Box 350122, Brooklyn, NY 11235-2525, USA
Tel: (718) 332-8336
Fax: (718) 646-2686
Email: wcfodogs@aol.com
Web: www.worldcaninefreestyle.org

HEALTH

UK

Alternative Veterinary Medicine Centre
Chinham House, Stanford in the Vale,
Oxfordshire, SN7 8NQ
Tel: 01367 710324
Fax: 01367 718243
Web: www.alternativevet.org/

British Small Animal Veterinary Association
Woodrow House, 1 Telford Way,
Waterwells Business Park, Quedgeley,
Gloucestershire, GL2 2AB
Tel: 01452 726700
Fax: 01452 726701
Email: customerservices@bsava.com
Web: http://www.bsava.com/

Royal College of Veterinary Surgeons
Belgravia House, 62-64 Horseferry Road,
London, SW1P 2AF
Tel: 0207 222 2001

Fax: 0207 222 2004
Email: admin@rcvs.org.uk
Web: www.rcvs.org.uk

USA

American Holistic Veterinary Medical Association
2218 Old Emmorton Road
Bel Air, MD 21015
Tel: 410 569 0795
Fax 410 569 2346
Email: office@ahvma.org
Web: www.ahvma.org/

American Veterinary Medical Association
1931 North Meacham Road, Suite 100,
Schaumburg, IL 60173-4360, USA.
Tel: 800 248 2862
Fax: 847 925 1329
Web: www.avma.org

American College of Veterinary Surgeons
19785 Crystal Rock Dr, Suite 305
Germantown, MD 20874, USA.
Tel: 301 916 0200
Toll Free: 877 217 2287
Fax: 301 916 2287
Email: acvs@acvs.org
Web: www.acvs.org/

AUSTRALIA

Australian Holistic Vets
Web: www.ahv.com.au/

Australian Small Animal Veterinary Association
40/6 Herbert Street, St Leonards, NSW 2065, Australia.
Tel: 02 9431 5090
Fax: 02 9437 9068
Email: asava@ava.com.au
Web: www.asava.com.au

Australian Veterinary Association
Unit 40, 6 Herbert Street, St Leonards,
NSW 2065, Australia.
Tel: 02 9431 5000
Fax: 02 9437 9068
Web: www.ava.com.au

Australian College Veterinary Scientists
Building 3, Garden City Office Park,
2404 Logan Road, Eight Mile Plains,
Queensland 4113, Australia.
Tel: 07 3423 2016
Fax: 07 3423 2977
Email: admin@acvs.org.au
Web: http://acvsc.org.au

ASSISTANCE DOGS

Canine Partners
Mill Lane, Heyshott, Midhurst,
, GU29 0ED
Tel: 08456 580480
Fax: 08456 580481
Web: www.caninepartners.co.uk

Dogs for the Disabled
The Frances Hay Centre, Blacklocks Hill,
Banbury, Oxon, OX17 2BS
Tel: 01295 252600
Web: www.dogsforthedisabled.org

Guide Dogs for the Blind Association
Burghfield Common, Reading, RG7 3YG
Tel: 01189 835555
Fax: 01189 835433
Web: www.guidedogs.org.uk/

Hearing Dogs for Deaf People
The Grange, Wycombe Road, Saunderton,
Princes Risborough, Bucks, HP27 9NS
Tel: 01844 348100
Fax: 01844 348101
Web: www.hearingdogs.org.uk

Pets as Therapy
3a Grange Farm Cottages, Wycombe Road,
Saunderton, Princes Risborough,
Bucks, HP27 9NS
Tel: 01845 345445
Fax: 01845 550236
Web: http://www.petsastherapy.org/

Support Dogs
21 Jessops Riverside, Brightside Lane,
Sheffield, S9 2RX
Tel: 01142 617800
Fax: 01142 617555
Email: supportdogs@btconnect.com
Web: www.support-dogs.org.uk

USA

Therapy Dogs International
88 Bartley Road, Flanders, NJ 07836,.
Tel: 973 252 9800
Fax: 973 252 7171
Email: tdi@gti.net
Web: www.tdi-dog.o

Therapy Dogs Inc.
P.O. Box 20227, Cheyenne, WY 82003.
Tel: 307 432 0272.
Fax: 307-638-2079
Web: www.therapydogs.com

Delta Society - Pet Partners
875 124th Ave NE, Suite 101 • Bellevue,
WA 98005 USA.
Email: info@DeltaSociety.org
Web: www.deltasociety.org

Comfort Caring Canines
8135 Lare Street, Philadelphia, PA 19128.
Email: ccc@comfortcaringcanines.org
Web: www.comfortcaringcanines.org/

AUSTRALIA

AWARE Dogs Australia, Inc
PO Box 883, Kuranda, Queensland, 488,
Australia.
Tel: 07 4093 8152
Web: www.awaredogs.org.au/

Delta Society -- Therapy Dogs
Web: www.deltasociety.com.au